Portraits for Fabric Lovers

Mastering the Technique of Realism

Marilyn Belford

Miriam's Dance (Homage to Hodler)

Front cover image taken from: *My Parents*
Back cover image taken from: *Rundy*

Every effort has been made to make sure the information and instruction provided in this book is accurate. It is presented in good faith, but no warranty is given and no results guaranteed. Since the author has no control over the choice of materials or procedures used, the author assumes no responsibility for the results and shall have no liability with respect to any loss or damage caused directly or indirectly by the information provided in this book.

All quilt photos in Chapter 11 are courtesy of the individual artists.

Terms mentioned in this book that are known trademarks have been appropriately capitalized and are trademarks of their respective owners.

You may order this book online. Copies of this book are also available at quantity discounts. For more information visit www.MarilynBelford.com/portraitbook/

In loving memory of my husband,
Julius Belford

Heartfelt thanks go out to all who helped bring this book to life, from those who read this manuscript in its various forms and offered comments to those who gave encouragement when it was most needed. Thanks also to my many students who took my classes and expressed their great appreciation for my teaching.

A very special thanks goes to Rundy, technical assistant extraordinaire, without whom this book could not have existed.

Contents

Introduction

Is This Book For You?

You do not need to know how to draw to make a good portrait in fabric.

You do not need to be an artist. The process of creating a fabric portrait requires no paint at all. The realistic effect is achieved strictly with fabric, repositionable fusible web and thread painting. With the step-by-step help provided in this book you will learn how to select a workable photograph, use the computer to enhance the photograph, choose and apply fabric, bring the portrait to life with thread painting, and complete all of the final touches. With this book you can successfully produce a fabric portrait that you will be proud to hang in your home.

I have met so many people who see portrait quilts and say they could not do it because they did not know how to draw or because they were not artistic enough. This is simply not true. It does not matter if you cannot draw a straight line. It does not matter if you think you do not have an artistic bone in your body. If you have a sewing machine and are comfortable using it, this book is for you.

I love creating fabric quilt portraits and I wrote this book so that everyone can enjoy creating a portrait quilt. It is my hope that *Portraits for Fabric Lovers* will help people everywhere realize that they, too, can do it.

What Is In This Book

Portraits for Fabric Lovers tackles every aspect of producing a fabulous fabric portrait. Instructions are detailed and step-by-step so no one will feel at a loss as to where to start or how to proceed.

Each chapter is focused on one or two main features. Then I break these down into the various steps so nothing will feel overwhelming. In the appropriate places I offer various techniques allowing you to find the method most compatible and comfortable for your needs. Each step is well illustrated so you can easily understand what is required.

To begin with, you will learn which photographs work best for translation into a realistic fabric portrait and how to avoid the pitfalls of starting with a poor picture. As you progress through the book you will discover various ways of enhancing your photograph through the use of your computer, making it so much easier for you to decide where to place your fabric pieces. After your photograph is prepared, you will learn the various methods of getting your photograph drawn onto muslin in life-like size.

Assembling your fabric portrait is an exciting time. There are several chapters filled with detailed instructions for everything involved in bringing your portrait together, from the first piece of fabric to the last stitch. With your fabric portrait constructed, there is only the finishing steps left. Once it is quilted, you will learn how to hang your quilt for everyone to admire. Done, and you said you couldn't do it!

A Last Word of Encouragement

I always tell my students, "Don't worry–it will only ruin all your fun." Losing the fear of "ruining the portrait" is the best antidote to actually ruining it. So don't worry. Creating a fabric portrait is intimidating at first–even I was nervous when I first started–but experience will give you confidence. Remember; you can do it.

Don't listen to the whisper of the inner critic who says you are not good enough. People have told me they couldn't do it, and then I watched them take my class and surprise even themselves by what they accomplished. Follow the instructions in this book and surprise yourself.

For encouragement and inspiration I urge you to flip to the back of the book and look at chapter eleven's gallery of quilts. You will see quilts there created by people who said "I can never make a realistic fabric portrait."

It is my hope that the techniques taught in this book will open new worlds for you to explore. Always remember that this is a learning process, and relax. Most of all, enjoy.

Marilyn Belford

Chapter 1
Choosing Your Photograph

Choosing the subject for a portrait quilt can be fun, or a bit tricky. When I decided to do a portrait quilt of my husband, Jules, he did not want me to do it. I wanted a good photograph on which to base my quilt, but he declined to be helpful. I had to follow him around the house with my camera, snapping shots of him whenever he turned around to snarl at me, or smirk disdainfully at my efforts. After awhile his eyes began to twinkle with amusement over my antics. Finally, he added a slight smile as if to say, "All right, take a photo of me if you must, but you are really annoying and I don't approve of this."

I always tell people this is the reason for the peculiar quality of my quilt portrait of Jules; depending on how the lighting strikes the portrait his expression will change. Sometimes he looks almost as if he is laughing at me. Other times, he seems to be frowning down with irritable severity. This depth of emotion (not to mention its variability!) brings life to the portrait, adding interest the quilt otherwise would not possess.

Hopefully, you will not be forced to chase your spouse around the house in the effort of acquiring a good photo for the basis of your quilt, but even without that difficulty, your choice of photograph requires care. The photograph you choose as the basis of your portrait quilt is, in a sense, the foundation upon which your quilt is built. For this reason it is necessary to take care in selecting the photograph that you will base your quilt on. A poor photograph will make the quilt portrait that much more difficult to create.

What is a good photograph for making a portrait quilt? That is the question this chapter will answer.

Choosing a Suitable Photograph

Numerous students have come to my classes with photographs not suitable for making into a portrait quilt. The problems have varied from photograph to photograph: Some were too vague, others were too washed out, and some were too small. Difficult photos abound, but with a little care the troubles can be avoided. The following ten points will guide you in the selection of your photograph.

1. Do not choose a young face for your first portrait quilt. The photograph below, as charming as it is, would be a poor choice. For the novice portrait-maker, a young face is difficult to thread paint because the skin is smooth. If you are not careful, a child's face can look a bit like a young Frankenstein's monster, all stitched up.

Fig. 1-1 A baby's face is very smooth

2. Choose a mature face for the first portrait quilt you do. This example would be a good choice. Notice how the face is not smooth. A mature face with wrinkles and shadows is quite forgiving as a subject matter, allowing ample room for creativity.

Fig. 1-2 Lots of wrinkles to play with

3. Avoid using a very small photograph. While it is technically possible to enlarge wallet size photographs, this is an added hassle and the results are always poorer than if a larger image was used to begin with. The photobelow is a poor choice. Enlarged, the photo would appear slightly blurred, and a lack of detail would become evident.

Fig. 1-3 Real size of photo is 1 ½" x 3 ½"

Fig. 1-4 Enlarged, face is blurred and pixelated

4. The photo you pick should be 3" x 5" or larger. The example given is of good size. It contains excellent detail and will scan into the computer well. Fig. 5 has unnecessary empty space but the image is large enough so that it can be cropped without the pixelation of the previous example.

Fig. 1-5. Old photo 3″ x 5″

Fig. 1-6 Now cropped and enlarged

5. Choose only one face for your first portrait quilt. Two faces require twice as much work as one, and three takes even more. Do not make your first portrait quilt hard for yourself. A photo such as Fig. 7 is more difficult and time consuming, a photo like Fig. 8 is good.

Fig. 1-7 Choose a simpler photograph

Fig. 1-8 A single face is easier

6. Do not choose a complex photograph. The example below has too much in the photograph. Some of the material is distracting, and other objects would be difficult to render. Attempting to make this photo into a quilt would likely be a frustrating experience.

7. A simple face shot, or at most, a bust length depiction is best. The example below is excellent. The subject matter is simple, well composed, and interesting.

Fig. 1-9 Much too complex for a first attempt

Fig. 1-10 Good composition

Fig. 1-11 Indistinct photo

8. Avoid photos that are indistinct, especially in areas that depict the shape of things, such as the shape of the head, nose, eyes, mouth and chin. This photograph does not show much of her features. There are few value levels giving you no shadows to work with.

9. A photo that has shadows that are too dark and too abrupt is difficult to work with. This photo has too much dark contrast. Half of the face is swallowed by deep shadow, and it is extremely difficult to see features or any subtleties. Delineated shadows are fine if they have good tones and values to play with.

Fig. 1-12 Photo too dark

Fig. 1-13 Photo with direct flash

10. A photograph taken head-on with a flash—such as the one on the left—is all right, but the shadows are difficult to work with and not compositionally exciting. Take care that the shadows cast by the flash do not create monster shapes in the background.

Judging Photographs

With the ten point list of things to avoid and look for in photographs you are ready to pick out the subject of your own quilt. Below are two example photographs to help you keep in mind what you are looking for.

This photograph of my mother and me is not bad. It has good value interest. The shadows are varied and well delineated. The only troublesome area is the outer hair shape of my mother. However, if this photograph were used it should not be difficult to adjust.

Fig. 15 is an excellent photograph. All edges are well defined. There is an abundance of value variation. The light source comes from the left and above.

It is helpful to remember that a photograph taken by a professional photographer is usually excellent to use because the photographer has great knowledge of light and dark, highlights and shadows, and strives for all the necessary diverse values in their photograph.

Fig. 1-14 Good lighting

Fig. 1-15 Excellent photograph

FAQ

Question:
I have a black and white photo, but would prefer to do a color portrait. Is it possible to do this?
Answer:
Using a black and white photo should be no problem as long as you know the subject's general coloring, i.e. is she blonde, does she have blue eyes, and is she fair, or have an olive complexion, etc. Also you can refer to photos other than the main black and white one you chose, when you are in doubt of something. Many of my students prefer the grayscale version of a photograph to play with because they feel that a posterized copy of a grayscale image is more distinct. However, you may find that if an area is indistinct then having color to refer to can help with decisions. The matter is a personal preference.

Question:
I have a photograph which contains extraneous stuff and unwanted objects. But I really like how the person in the photograph looks. Is there any way I can use this photo?
Answer:
It depends on how much of a distraction they are. If you have a photograph of a person that you want to use but the image has a lot of complex or distracting material you can consider cropping, covering over, or simply ignoring the unwanted items.

Question:
Can I use a photograph taken with a digital camera?
Answer:
Yes, so long as it is of sufficient quality. Most modern digital cameras can do an excellent job. If you have an older camera with a resolution lower than 2.0 megapixels, you may find that when the picture is enlarged the details are too fuzzy. An advantage of having a digital camera is it eliminates the step of scanning the photograph onto the computer.

Question:
I really want to do both of my parents in my portrait quilt. Can I make a smaller portrait of them so the finished quilt is still the same size? What if the faces are in the 6 to 8 inch range?
Answer:
Two faces are more work than one, and this is hard for a beginner. I suggest to my students that they try something easier as a first quilt. However, if you do make a quilt with two faces, keep their heads "human" size. The quilt will be larger, but the portraits will look more natural. One other consideration—the smaller the size of the head, the smaller the size of the fabric template. This makes the cutting of the fabric and its placement more difficult.

Chapter 2
Posterizing Your Photograph

What is Posterization?

Posterizing an image is sometimes called color simplification, or color reduction. In computer photo editing software this process reduces the number of colors in an image. The result shows colors and shadows separated into planes, as is seen in the comparison between the posterized and unposterized images below.

Fig. 2-1 Unposterized

Fig. 2-2 Posterized

The reason I have my students do this is not because I want their dear relative or friend to look ugly and blotchy, but because posterizing a photograph is a simple process that greatly aids the creation of a portrait quilt. To understand this, take a close look at the unposterized image on the left (Fig. 1). A normal photograph has thousands upon thousands of colors all mixed together, but after the posterization process the number of colors is reduced to various tone areas (Fig. 2). These tone areas can easily be created as fabric shapes for the portrait.

I strongly recommend my students follow the posterizing process described in this chapter. It is not a difficult procedure, and I give clear directions that even a computer novice can follow. If you do not have a computer, it is possible your local library might have the equipment. Or, if for whatever reason, you do not want to attempt to digitally posterize your photograph yourself, it is possible to have the work done for you at copy centers like OfficeMax, Office Depot, Kinkos, and similar places. Bring your photo and this book, and explain to them what you want done.

For those of you who cannot digitally posterize your photograph, and those of you who do not want to have someone else do it for you, then all you need to do is enlarge your photograph until the head of your portrait is approximately 8 - 8 ½" for a child, and for an adult, about 10" from the tip of the chin straight up to the top of the crown (skull). This can easily be done at a copy center or similar location. Use as light a weight paper as possible, as this will help in the tracing process later on.

Preparing For Posterization

The first step is getting your photograph onto the computer. If the photo you want to use is a digital picture already on your computer, your job is much easier. For those of you intending to use a photo that is not digital, you will need to scan it into the computer. It is best to scan your image at 600 dpi and no less that 300 dpi. If you're not sure how to set your scanning dpi, just do it at the default setting. It may not be perfect, but it will probably be adequate for the next step.

Once you have your photo on your computer, save two separate copies (Fig. 2-3). The best place to save your images is somewhere in your My Documents where you will not forget the location. Label one clearly as a backup and never modify this copy. The second copy will be the image you modify and work with. If somehow you ever mess up you can go back to your backup copy and make a fresh duplicate with which to work.

Software For Posterizing

Fig. 2-3 Saving your image

After you have scanned and saved your image it is time to posterize. Almost any photo editing program is sufficient. If you have a scanner or a digital camera and you installed image editing software that came with the program, you probably have a photo editing program that is capable of posterizing.

If you have no photo editing software, you can purchase some either on the internet or at a local store. Prices can vary widely, so it pays to shop around. Some companies offer free trial versions of their software for downloading from the internet, and there are even some full programs that are entirely free. However, the more popular programs that you find in the store are easiest to use.

Depending on the photo editing software you have, the location of the posterize effect will vary, as well as its name. The option to posterize may be called Posterize, Reduce Colors, Color Simplification, or something similar. This option is often found in a pull down menu such as Effects, or Image, Arrange, Transform, or Color.

I encourage you to experiment with the software. Play around. Photo software can do all sorts of interesting and exciting things to photographs that just might inspire you in your portrait quilt. Do not be hesitant or afraid. There is always an undo option, and you have a backup copy of your photo, just in case.

Posterizing Step-by-Step

As an example of how the process is done, I will give step by step instructions for doing posterizing using Jasc Paint Shop Pro. The process will be slightly different in other programs, but the idea and procedure is generally the same.

First, before I posterize my photo I smooth and then sharpen the image. This extra procedure is not required but I have found it helps produce a better posterized image.

To start, load up your image into Jasc Paint Shop Pro. Then click on the <u>Adjust</u> option, go down the menu and click on <u>Add/Remove Noise</u>. Go down the menu that pops out and click on <u>Edge Preserving Smooth . . .</u>

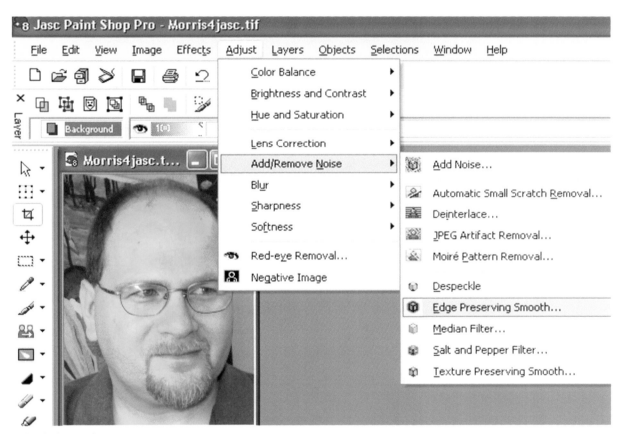

Fig. 2-4 The first step

Experiment with the amount of smoothing you use–you can always undo mistakes. The amount of smoothing required will vary from one image to another. You will know when you have it right when the image no longer has a grainy quality. Do not smooth an image too much, or the face will begin to lose distinguishing features. The purpose of smoothing is to make a cleaner posterized image. It is better to smooth too little rather than too much.

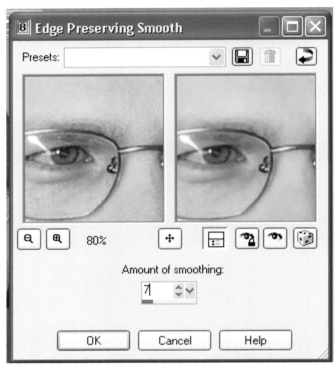

Fig. 2-5 Smoothing the image

After smoothing the image it is time to sharpen. In Jasc Paint Shop Pro you will find this feature by clicking on the <u>Adjust</u> option, then clicking on <u>Sharpness</u>, and then clicking <u>Sharpen</u>.

Fig. 2-6 Selecting sharpen

The goal of sharpening is to make the features of the face as clear as possible without the image becoming grainy. The amount of sharpening will vary from image to image. Sometimes it is best to sharpen several times slightly, rather than sharpening a lot just once.

After you have sharpened the image to your satisfaction, it is time to do the actual posterization. To posterize, click on the Effects option and go down to click on the Artistic Effects option. You will see a lot of choices. Go down the list and choose Posterize.

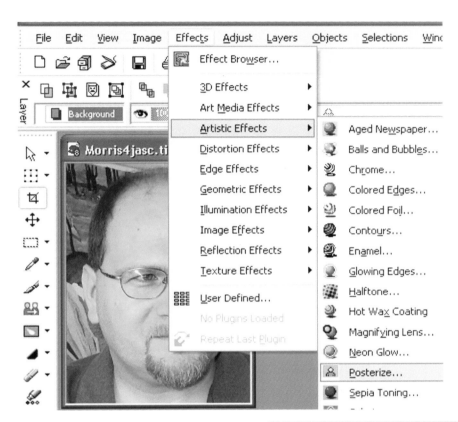

Fig. 2-7 Select posterize

When the posterize box opens play with the level of posterization that you want. You will know that you have arrived at the proper level of posterization when you can visualize cutting a fabric template from one of the separations of color. If you have too many little separations then you will find that you cannot easily cut a piece of fabric to that particular shape and size. This means you have to posterize the image further.

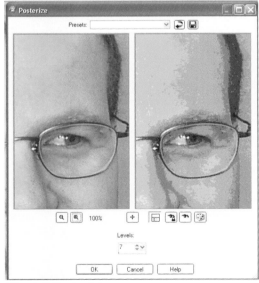

Fig. 2-8 Posterizing

Other Programs

There are many different photo editing programs available, and what works best for you is a matter of personal taste. If I tried to give directions for using every different photo software available, I could almost write a book just about that. If you are using software other than Jasc Paint Shop Pro, I am sure you can find the posterize feature (perhaps called color reduction or color level) in your particular software if you look around.

As an example, in SmartDraw Photo you would select the Image option, the click Special Effects and choose the posterize option. The layout is slightly different from Jasc Paint Shop, but the end result is the same.

Fig. 2-9 Posterizing in SmartDraw Photo

Posterizing to Perfection

I cannot give you a definitive level number since results vary according to program, color, and/or resolution.

Pay no attention to strange colors if they appear. When you make your quilt you will be following the colors of the original photograph. The objective of posterization is to split the colors into well demarcated areas. When you can visualize cutting a piece of fabric into the shapes you see, then you have probably arrived at the desired level of posterization.

Fig. 10 is an example of an image before it was posterized

The example below that (Fig. 11) is of an image not posterized enough. There are still too many colors. If you tried to cut a piece of cloth for every color, you would have a million little peices.

Fig. 12 was posterized much more strongly. It is very simplified in color and the areas are markedly separated. However, this image was posterized too much. It would be easy to trace the various shapes, but it has lost too much of the detail of the features.

The last (Fig. 13) shows an image that has been posterized just the right amount. The colors are clearly separated, but the details remain. It is much easier to trace the outlines of the features and shadows in this posterized image than in the original version.

Fig. 2-10 Pre-posterized

Fig. 2-12 Excessive

Fig. 2-11 Insufficient

Fig. 2-13 Perfect

With your photograph now properly posterized, save it under a different name than what your original photo was called.

FAQ

Question:
How can I save a backup copy of the image I scanned without scanning the image twice?
Answer:
You do not need to scan the image twice. When you load the image into your photo editing software click on the <u>File</u> menu and choose the option <u>Save As</u>. So long as you enter a new name for your image each time, you can make as many copies as you want.

Question:
What format should I use when saving my digital image?
Answer:
Do not use the .gif format because it can only save with 256 colors. Otherwise, you can use whatever format you prefer. Professionally, .tif is considered good because it saves images without any loss in quality. The .jpg format is commonly used, and is fine.

Question:
My posterized image looks ugly. How am I going to make a beautiful portrait out of this?
Answer:
The posterized image is only a grid upon which to base your drawing and templates. The actual construction with fabric and threadpainting is based upon the original photo.

Chapter 3
Tracing and Translation to Muslin

In this chapter we will trace our photograph and translate the line drawing to our muslin base. There are several ways you can do this procedure. The method you choose will depend on your taste, and which is best suited to your available supplies.

This is a three part process. The first step is preparing the posterized image for tracing. The second step is creating a line drawing from your photograph which will be the master template from which we work to create the quilt. The last step is translating the line drawing to your muslin so that you will know the shape of the fabric pieces you must cut. At this point you will be ready to begin the actual construction of the quilt.

Step One:
Preparing Image For Tracing

Method A: Projection

If your printer is capable of printing on transparency film and you have access to an overhead projector, this is the most convenient method for transferring.

It is a simple two step process of printing out the *posterized* version of your image onto the transparency that can then be projected onto the tracing paper for tracing.

When printing out on transparency film you will want to make sure you print out the image approximately 3" x 5" and no larger than 4" x 6". If you make the transparency more than 4" x 6", you will have to place the projector so close to the screen that you will have eliminated any space for you to stand by the screen to transfer the design. If the image on the

transparency is too small—smaller than 3" x 5"—the distance from the projector to the muslin will have to be fairly far, causing the lines (when projected) to become fuzzy.

If you need to resize your posterized image so that it is between 4" x 6" and 3" x

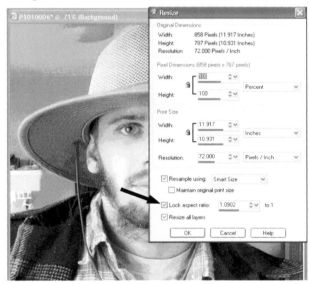

Fig. 3-1 Maintaining size ratio when **resizing**

5" make sure you keep the size ratio the same as the original image (Fig 3-1). Otherwise, the image will become distorted.

If you do not have the ability to print onto transparency film, or you do not have access to an overhead projector, you can print the posterized version of your photograph onto a 4" x 6" or 8" x 10" photo paper and bring it to a photo processing shop. They can make a slide from the photo which you can use for the projection of the image.

Method B: Enlargment

If you don't have access to either an overhead projector or a slide projector you can create a life size copy of your posterized image and trace this. What is a life sized copy? The average head measures approximately 8 1/2" -10" from the tip of the chin straight up to the top of the crown (skull). This means you will want to enlarge your line drawing until it is somewhere around this size.

In the finished fabric portrait, the head should be close to natural size. Why? I recommend life size proportions because the smaller the portrait the smaller the details, and the smaller the details the smaller the pieces you must handle, making it more difficult to manipulate. The reason you do not want to make an oversized head is because if the head is slightly larger than life it will look unnatural and wrong. The artist Chuck Close painted 8' heads. This was acceptable because he did it to produce a certain effect. If you are trying to produce a natural, realistic look, keep the portrait as close to human proportions as possible.

If your printer is capable of printing out the image at the proper enlargement, and you want to do it yourself, remember to keep the original size ratio, as I explained in the previous method. Otherwise your enlarged image will end up distorted.

Fig. 3-2 Rundy distorted

If you do not want to do the enlargement yourself you can bring a printout of the posterized image to a printing shop like Kinko's and have them enlarge it to a life sized copy on ordinary paper.

Step Two: Creating The Line Drawing

First, set up your foamcore board, or insulation board in the location where you intend to work on your quilt. Depending on the size of your house or apartment, you might not have much choice, but a well lit location that allows you to place the board in an upright position is best. I use my dining room buffet top to brace my board. I walk by that area often and can glance at my work in progress while doing other chores. It is surprising how many problems get solved when you are not concentrating on them. I secure the board to the wall with masking tape to make sure it will not move out of position.

How you proceed from here depends on whether you are following method A or method B.

If Following Method A: Projection

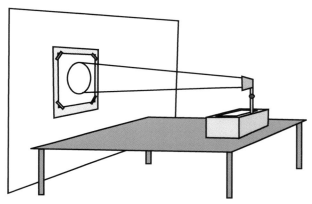

Fig. 3-3 Projector setup

With drafting tape (an artist's tape that is less tacky than masking tape), attach a sheet of tracing paper that is slightly larger than the intended portrait to your insulation board. Tape only enough to keep the tracing paper from shifting. Now project your transparency film onto the tracing paper.

Play with the size you want the picture to be by projecting it onto the board and moving the projector closer and further away and focusing each time. Measure the desired size.

With the transparency superimposed on the tracing paper, you can trace out the shapes in your photograph with a pencil.

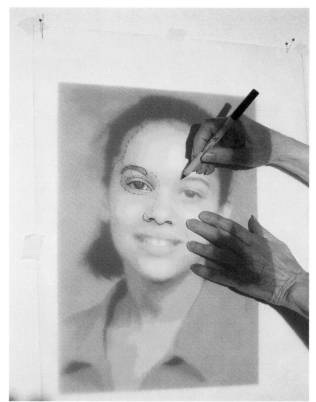

Fig. 3-4 Tracing projected image onto tracing paper

This is where the posterization of your image helps. With the colors separated out you can easily follow the various shapes.

If you feel sure-handed you can use the Ultra-fine Sharpie at this point and save yourself some time. When using a pencil

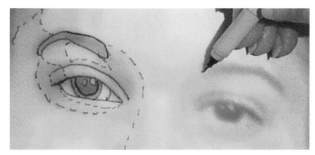

Fig. 3-5 Tracing the shape of things

make sure it is sharpened so that it makes a clear mark, but not so sharp that it tears the tracing paper.

The projection will be slightly fuzzy, even at the best focus. This is not unsurmountable. Draw your line with the

pencil (or Sharpie marker) right down the middle of the fuzz.

I like to draw distinct facial features with a solid line, and shadows or transitional shifts with a dotted line. You can use a different color pencil or pen (such as red) instead of the dashed lines. If you

Fig. 3-6 Example line drawing with solid and dashed lines

Fig. 3-7 Close up of line drawing

draw everything in black solid lines, it will be like getting lost on a crowded subway. It is important to be fairly detailed for this part, but be careful that the areas outlined are not too small to be cut from fabric.

If your line strays slightly off the center do not worry. It does not make much difference in the final result.

When you have finished, if you used a pencil like me, you will now have to retrace the pencil line with your Ultra-fine Sharpie. This will give it a nice crisp, clear line that will never smear nor fade and remains distinctive even when dark fabric lies underneath.

What you have completed on the tracing paper is what I call the mastercopy. From this you will create your quilt.

As you work on your line drawing and later on the quilt, it is good to keep a print of the original photograph near the area on which you are working for reference. If possible, sometimes it is good to even have several different photographs of the portrait subject on hand. Why? Sometimes a section or a feature of the face is unclear on the photograph you have selected to copy. It is then possible to refer to another photo to help you decide what you want to do. For example, if I see a dark spot near the corner

of an eye, but it is unclear to me whether it is a wrinkle, mole or shadow. I look at the other photo and see that the dark spot is actually just a shadow. I then decide that I do not want to use that shadow and will eliminate it from my portrait altogether.

Having finished this step, you will have no further need of the overhead projector or slide projector.

Remove the tape holding the tracing paper in place. Be careful not to tear the paper. Remove the tracing paper from the foamboard.

If Following Method B: Enlargement

If you are working from an enlarged (life size) posterized image the process is still very much similar to the projection of method A. Read the instructions for method A so that you understand the technique. The only difference is that instead of tracing from the projected image you will be tracing from the enlarged image to create the line drawing mastercopy.

There are two ways you can do this. The easier method is to take acetate paper—which is clear—and lay it over your enlarged posterized image and trace with a Sharpie Ultra-fine pen. Acetate paper is not to be mistaken for transparency film which is used with the overhead projector. Transparency film for the overhead projector is 8 ½" by 11" and is used with a printer and projector. Acetate paper comes in various sizes. You will need to purchase some large enough to hold your traced image. Acetate paper is difficult to transfer through to the muslin underneath. Instead, you could use a thin clear vinyl which can be purchased very inexpensively at craft stores. It is softer, more pliable, and allows pencil pressure to transfer nicely.

Fig. 3-8 Lots of photos around work area

The second option is to use tracing paper and create a light box. To do this, choose a window not in direct sunlight and tape the enlarged posterized copy of your image onto the window pane. Make sure your photo is facing toward you. Otherwise, if the photo is reversed it will not look like the person, or at least it will look peculiar.

Once you have the photo taped to the window, tape a sheet of tracing paper over the enlargement, securing it so that it will not shift. You now have a home made light box.

Using a soft (2B) pencil, trace the outline and shapes, just as instructed in method A.

Fig. 3-9 Homemade light box

Fig. 3-10 Example of dealing with pixilation

Dealing With Pixilation

Posterizing never turns out perfect. In working with your posterized image you have probably noticed the pixilated blocky appearance of the colors in your posterized image. Don't worry about this. The solution in dealing with those pesky jagged edges is to ignore them. Follow the general shape of the various colors and ignore the tiny jagged variations. This will give you a nice smooth shape to cut out later.

Some shapes are too small to cut out of fabric. Don't bother with such very small sections. Omit them. Some lines are too narrow for fabric as well. If they are important to the structure of the portrait, mark them on your line drawing and they can be thread painted on the quilt later.

What If I Couldn't Posterize?

If for some reason you could not posterize your image you can still follow whichever of the above methods you choose for creating your line drawing. The problem you will face is that without the posterization of your image the colors of the photograph will not be separated into sections. You will have to use your own eye to estimate where the various shapes should follow.

A posterized image is much preferred as it makes tracing the mastercopy line drawing much easier.

Transferring To A Muslin Foundation

Take your prewashed and ironed muslin and cut it 1 ½" or preferably larger all around than your desired finished portrait top section (without the border). Tape the cut muslin to your foamcore board (from herein simply called the "board"). If tape will not stick to the board, then pin the muslin down to it. Most insulation board is 5/8" thick. I gently turn the muslin over the edge and stick pins into the sides. Do not stretch the muslin too tight, it could skew the image when unstretched. Just make sure it is laying smooth.

If your board is much larger than the piece of muslin being used, or if you are using foamboard (thinner than insulation board) then just pin or tape down the edges of the muslin onto the front of the board.

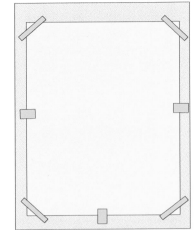
Fig. 3-12 Muslin taped to foamboard

Place your master copy over the muslin and tape it down across the top edge only, so that you can flip the paper to view the muslin underneath and to later apply your pieces of fabric to the muslin.

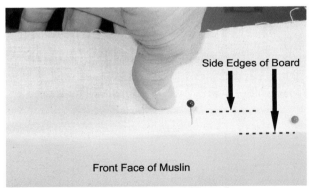
Side Edges of Board

Front Face of Muslin

Fig. 3-11 Pin muslin over edge of board

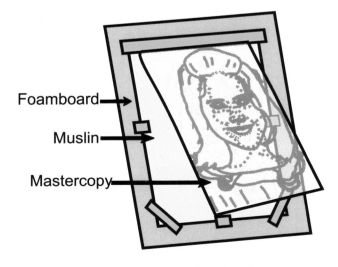
Foamboard

Muslin

Mastercopy

Fig. 3-13 Mastercopy can be flipped

It is now time to transfer your master copy onto the muslin base. Place a piece of transfer paper under the tracing paper, securing it in place on top of the muslin. Trace the design onto the muslin using a not overly sharp pencil.

Do not press too hard on the pencil,

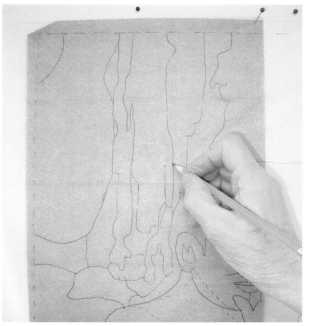

Fig. 3-14 Transfer drawing onto muslin

just enough to distinguish the lines lightly on the muslin. The light lines left by the transfer paper are used as reference points for where to apply the fabric. You do not want to make them too dark on the chance they might show through light colored, light weight fabric.

When you have finished tracing onto the muslin do not untape the master copy. This stays on for reference all through the applique work.

In the next chapter I will guide you through the process of picking out fabric for your quilt.

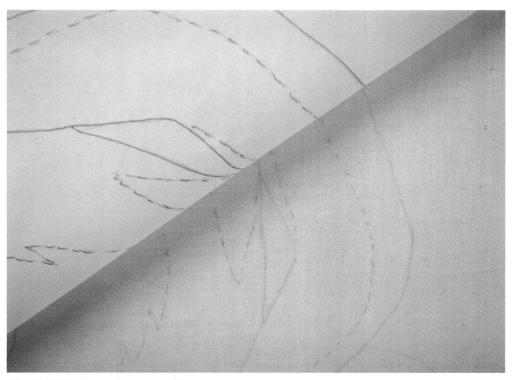

Fig. 3-15 Light marks on muslin

FAQ

Question:
Is it easier to use a grayscale photo for tracing than a color photo?

Answer:
It is a matter of preference. Some claim that using values alone makes it easier to follow. I like to use color because if the values are close, I can distinguish the separation by the difference in color.

Question:
You can see everything when using vinyl or acetate paper, why would anyone want to use tracing paper?

Answer:
Some find that the tracing paper softens the image underneath because it is translucent rather than transparent and thus reduces the distraction of details, making it easier to retrace a section for the template. It is also lighter weight and easier to manipulate. And it is much less expensive.

Chapter 4
Line Drawings

You may create your line drawing using the methods described in the previous chapter. I prefer to use a vector program like CorelDraw. In this chapter I will show you how to create a line drawing on the computer. Those of you who have a vector drawing program may choose to use this method. I will be demonstrating in CorelDraw, however, there are many vector drawing programs—for example, Adobe Illustrator.

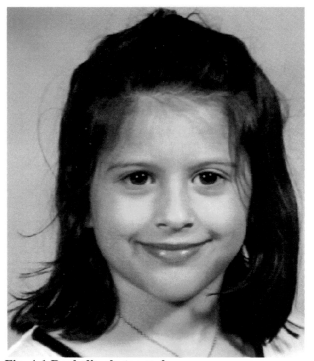

Fig. 4-1 Rachel's photograph

Fig. 4-2 Rachel posterized

To begin, posterize your image as described in chapter two. For this demonstration I will be using a photograph of my granddaughter Rachel. Notice the nicely posterized image of Rachel on the right.

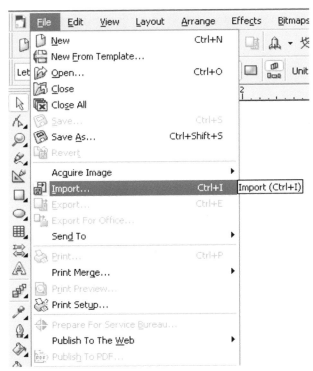

Fig. 4-3 Importing image

Step 1

    After posterizing your image, you want to Import it into your vector drawing program. In CorelDraw the Import feature is found under the File menu.

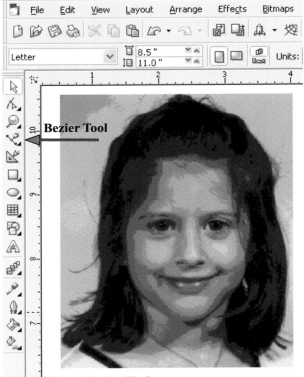

Bezier Tool

Fig. 4-4 Select Bezier Tool

Step 2

    Once your image is imported, you are ready to start your line drawing. The tool you will be using is called the Bezier Tool.

    This tool creates a line between points. Each point along the line is called a node. These nodes can be adjusted to modify the shape of the line.

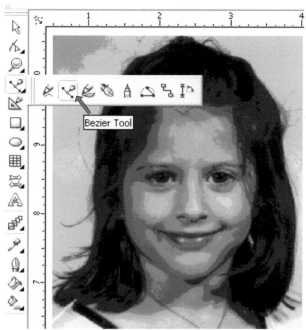

Fig. 4-5 Pullout menu

Step 2 Continued

In CorelDraw the Bezier Tool is found within the pullout tab for the <u>Drawing Tools</u> (see Fig. 5).

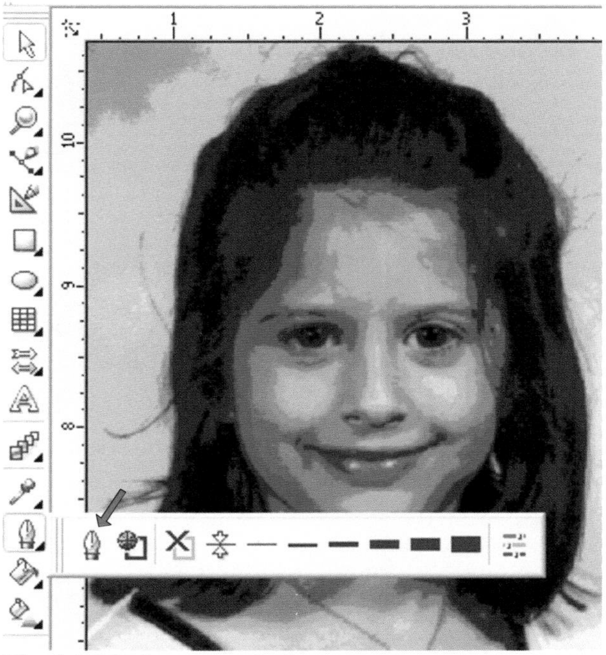

Fig. 4-6 Click pen symbol

Step 3

Once you have selected the Bezier Tool, you need to set the line properties. Click on the <u>Outline Tool</u> to open a dialog box.

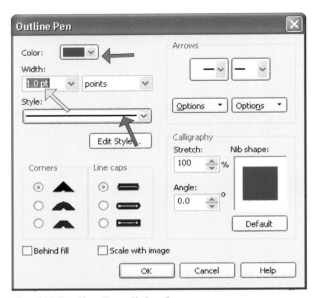
Fig. 4-7 Outline Pen dialog box

Step 3 Continued

When I create my line drawings I prefer to use a blue line. Bright blue is not a natural skin tone so it is more visible than a black line which can disappear into hair and other dark areas.

A 1.0 pt. line is a good thickness. Anything thinner will be too indistinct for projection. Anything thicker than 2.0 pt. will obscure the finer details.

Select a solid line for the main features of the face.

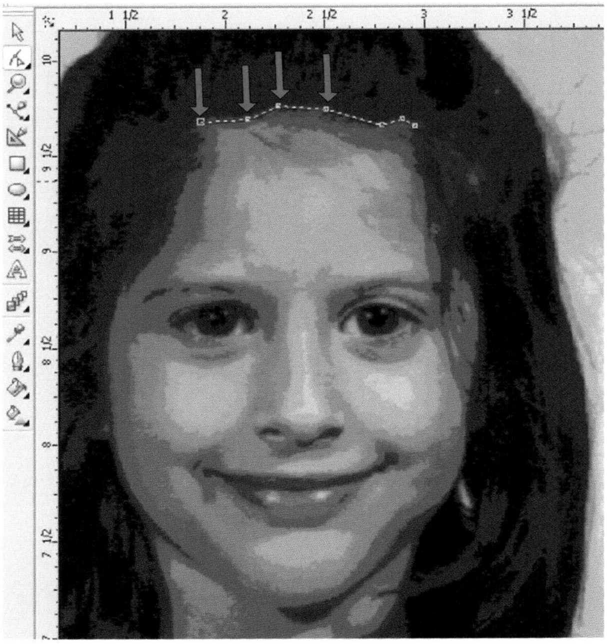

Step 4

Once your Tool is set as described above, begin drawing your lines. Starting at the hairline, draw your line following the shape of the face by clicking a new node for every change of direction.

Continue drawing in this fashion until the main features such as the eyes, nose, mouth, ears, and hair are complete.

Fig. 4-8 Creating line nodes

Fig. 4-9 Solid lines for main features

Fig. 4-10 Main features drawn

Step 5

Once the features are finished, you can turn your attention to the shadows and color changes in the face. This is best done with a dashed line.

Go back into the outline dialog box and select one of the dotted lines. I prefer a medium dotted line.

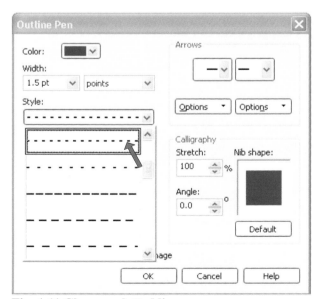

Fig. 4-11 Choose a dotted line

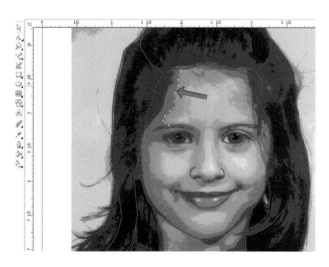

Fig. 4-12 Dotted lines for shadows

Fig. 4-13 Overlayed images

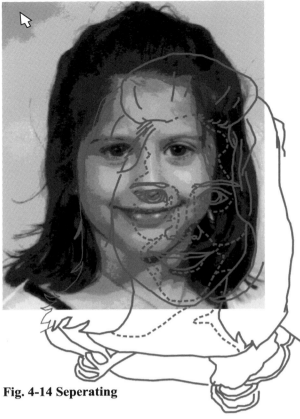

Fig. 4-14 Seperating

Fig. 4-15 Finished line drawing

Using the dotted line, draw all the shadows and color changes into individual complete shapes capable of being cut out. You will be using these shapes as guides for cutting out pieces of fabric.

Once your line drawing is complete (Fig. 13), you need to separate the posterized image from the line drawing. To do this, grab the corner of your posterized image with the mouse cursor (you must be out of the Bezier drawing mode) and drag the photo out from under the line drawing. Make sure you do not select the line drawing as well.

Save the line drawing. Print out the line drawing and bring it into a copy center and have them enlarge the printout so that the head measures (from chin to crown) measures 10 to 10 ½ inches for an adult. From this enlarged image, make a tracing onto tracing paper or clear vinyl. This will be your mastercopy, as described in chapter three.

If you prefer, you may instead create a transparency of your line drawing and project it onto the tracing paper.

Chapter 5
Fabric Choices

I adore shopping for fabric. When I go shopping in a fabric store its like entering a fairy tale land. When I look at fabrics I don't see ordinary patterns or colors, I see beards, hair, water, sky, angry sky, calm sky. I see young skin, I see an old man's forehead. I see gray curly hair. I see five o'clock shadow, I see chin stubble. If I'm shopping with a friend I will sometimes hear a shout from behind a stack of fabric calling me to come look at the perfect hair fabric.

This will be a new way of looking at fabric for you. When I arrive at the counter ready to pay, my stack of bolts looks strange to most bystanders. Nothing really matches. Guiltily, I explain that I do pictorial quilts and that's the reason for the melange of strange color combinations. I often wonder if that explanation helps. They still look at me strangely.

In this chapter I will give you some guiding principles to help you in the process of choosing your fabric. The choice of fabric is a very personal thing, much like an artist's choice of color mixtures. There are no rules about what fabric you must use, but I can help you see fabric in a new way, and give you suggestions to guide you in your own choices.

When you step into the fabric store remember, above all else, to be creative. Don't limit yourself. Don't buy one skin color of different values, purchase several tones! Light mauves, light olives are good for shadows.

Buy prints that appear as a solid color from a few feet away, but at a closer inspection are not (Fig. 5-1 to the right).

Fig. 5-1 Same fabric as seen from a distance and on the right, closeup

In the two samples below (Fig. 5-2 and 5-3) you can see how this works in the portrait of *My Parents.*

Batiks that shift colors are good too, as well as marbelized fabric, and fossil ferns. You need a great variety and supply of smallish pieces of fabric from which to choose when bringing your fabric portrait to life.

Fig. 5-3 Viewed up close

Fig. 5-2 Seen from a distance

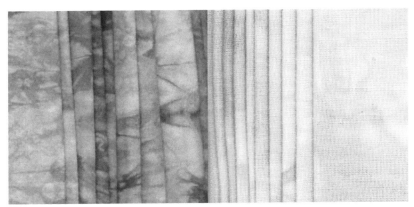

Fig. 5-4 Various good fabric selections

Gradual color shifting will add greater realism to your work. For example, using fabric that shifts from a natural skin tone to an olive hue is good for shading in such areas as under the eye. It helps provide a smooth color shift without an added seam.

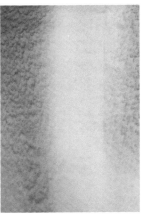
Fig. 5-5 Soft color shifts

Fig. 5-6 Marbelized batik

Fig. 5-7 Another batik

Fig. 5-8 Fossil fern fabric

Fig. 5-9 More fossil fern fabric

Note the various textures and tones. This is good. The greater the variety you can use the more interest is incorporated into the portrait.

Hair

It is good to think creatively when you are looking for fabric which can function as hair in your quilt portrait. Some of the fabric below was cat hair from a cat fabric print. The following fabrics are good for hair.

Fig. 5-10 Assorted fabric for hair

The first time I used a cat fur pattern for hair I had to close my eyes before I could cut the cute kitty cat into smithereens. Not all of your hair must come from animal prints. Look around for various wavy and lined designs. Patterns of wood grain are marvelous, as are marbelized swirls.

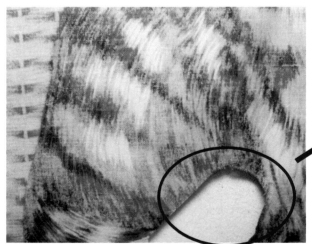

Fig. 5-11 Wrong side of cat fabric

Fig. 5-12 Jules' hair

These two examples show how I fussycut a piece of the backside of cat fabric to make the hair on Jules, my husband.

Fig. 5-13 Photograph of Morris

Fig. 5-14 Quilt of Morris

Morris, my son, is a fair complexioned man with light hair on his chest. I searched long and hard for the right fabric to portray the visible chest hair at the opening of his shirt. Some fabric does not resemble hair at all, but, from a distance works very well as hair. The fabric example below shows how I used such a fabric in my quilt *Morris*. I searched until I found the perfect swirling pattern in a print of fabric. Up close you can see the swirly design that makes the hair.

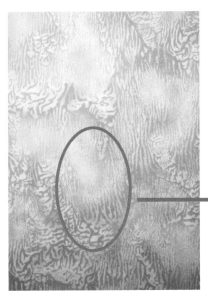

Fig. 5-15 Fabric for chest hairs

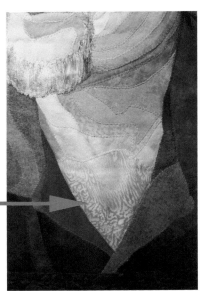

Fig. 5-16 Fabric as applied in portrait

Another consideration is to make sure it can blend smoothly into the skin so that it looks like hair growing out of the skin. To this end I fussycut a piece that includes an area without the swirls.

When I choose the fabric for the faces in my portraits, I always try to keep in mind the emotional quality I want to convey. For example, when I was putting together the quilt portrait of my son Marty I went down to the fabric shop and first browsed through the different sections that I think is skin color. I looked at the peach tones, I looked at the pink tones, I looked at the beige tones. I eliminated the pink tones, especially those that have a lot of blue in them, mainly because he has dark hair, brooding eyes, and a medium complexion.

Fig. 5-17 Original photo of Marty

Fig. 5-18 Fabrics used for Marty

Subtle shifting is good when you want to make a cheek that has a slight glow in the center where light is reflecting, or when you want to move from one section to another with only one "seam."

Some people who are new to quilt portraits stick to solid colors. Solid colors are okay, but they can be boring. There are enough batiks with widely spaced areas within them and printed fabrics that read as textured solids that you do not have to resort to simply solid colors.

Fig. 5-19 Note shifting batiks on forehead and cheek

Don't be afraid to use fairly strong prints. I say fairly strong because you don't want the prints to be too strong. What I mean by not too strong is no distinct shapes that call attention to themselves.

Sometimes I find that reversing a fabric and using its back side instead, can help add variation. Reversing in this manner can give a smooth shift of values.

Fig. 5-20 Some areas are too heavily marked

Fig. 5-21 Front and reverse of fabric

Fig. 5-22 Reverse fabrics for folds in shirt

Notice the excellent effect achieved by the use of the front and back of the same fabric on Rundy's shirt.

When working on your portrait it is nice to have a wide variety of fabrics to choose from. However, if you find that you are missing something, you can always go out and buy more fabric selections halfway through a project. Sometimes I have had to do this. Above all, experiment. Discover what works for you. There is a wealth of fabric types and patterns out there. You won't find one "right" type of fabric, only endless possibilities.

When you step into the fabric store remember that there is material for every shade, every hue, and every pattern—for those willing to look. Tell yourself this, and then go for it!

Chapter 6
Fusible Web

Now that you have picked out your photo, posterized it (if you were going to), completed your line drawing, and collected some of your fabric, you are ready to dive right in and begin putting your quilt together. This is where the real fun begins. This is when all your hard work begins to show results.

In this chapter I will explain how to use fusible web. In the following chapter I will walk you through the process of auditioning pieces of fabric for your portrait, and putting it together. You will need to read over both chapters once before you get started, and then refer back to various sections as needed.

Fusible Web

The main purpose for the use of fusible web in my approach is to keep exposed edges of fabric from fraying and to allow for sewing without pins. Fusible web can, however, add some stiffness to the finished product. For this reason I prefer Steam-A-Seam 2 Lite since it does not make bulky buildup, and I can overlay several layers of fabric smoothly. When purchasing Steam-A-Seam 2 Lite, make sure it is just that. The "2" in the name means that the material is tacky on *both* sides. The "Lite" on the package distinguishes it from its sister product which is much heavier and thicker in texture and *will* make the quilt stiff.

Most double-sided webs come sandwiched between two layers of an adhesive-resistant paper. When not in use, always keep fusible webs sealed well in plastic, such as a Ziploc bag, or it may become dried out. If it does, it sometimes reconstitutes its tackiness if you lightly steam it. Sometimes just breathing on it like a dragon works. Or, you can iron the piece of fabric before cutting the shape and sticking the warm fabric onto the tacky webbing. Whatever you do, *do not iron the Steam-a-Seam 2!* If steaming does not help, spray just a little bit of temporary adhesive spray on the back of the fabric before applying it to the webbing. This disappears with time.

When fusing, always follow the manufacturer's directions.

With the use of the double-sided web, it is comforting to know that all during the fabric application, nothing is permanent. You can remove your choice and replace it at any time during the process until you steam iron it into place. This should take away any fear you may have about making a wrong decision as you try out fabric on your quilt.

Using Your Templates

Remember the "mastercopy" that you made in the last chapter? Now is the time you will use it. From this mastercopy you will trace out templates for each individual section of fabric. By using this method you will get fabric pieces in exactly the size and shape you want, without a lot of hassle and frustration.

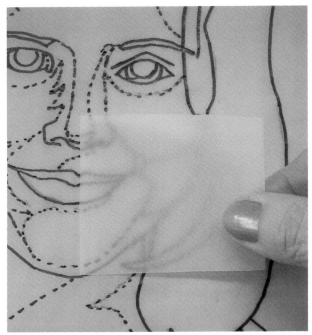

Fig. 6-1 Placing the tracing paper

To make templates for each section, cut a piece of tracing paper slightly larger than the selected section. Place on top of the mastercopy.

I then trace the section using a fine point marker. Notice at the red arrow that I have followed the exact line of the mastercopy which indicates the edge of the face. The blue arrow shows that I have drawn in a scant 1/4" allowance for the adjoining pieces to overlap.

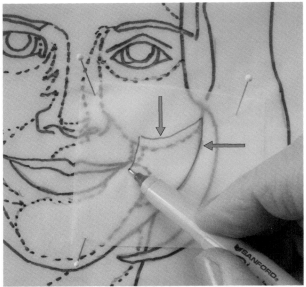

Fig. 6-2 Tracing a template.

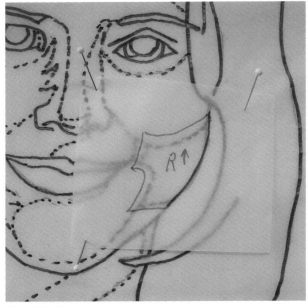

Fig. 6-3 Completed tracing

Hunt out the section of the fabric you like (fussy selecting) and pin the traced template to the **right** side.

Fig. 6-4 Fussy-select and pin to right side of fabric

Although it may be considered wasteful, I like to cut out a manageable piece to work with.

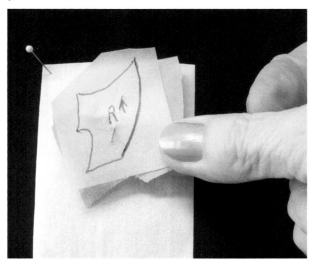

Fig. 6-5 Measure and cut a piece of Steam-a-Seam 2 Lite

From a sheet of Steam-A-Seam 2 Lite I cut a section large enough to cover the tracing paper.

Steam-A-Seam 2 Lite comes between two layers of non-adhesive backing. Separate one layer of the backing from the web, whichever side comes away easier.

Fig. 6-6 Peel off one side

Place the fabric and tracing paper template onto the **tacky** side of the Lite. Notice the R on the tracing paper which I added to indicate that right side of the template so that it always remains up.

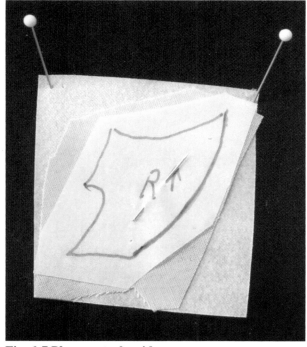

Fig. 6-7 Place on tacky side

Now cut out the traced shape through all the layers. If your piece is small enough, you don't have to re-pin through all the layers. The tackiness of the web holds it well in place.

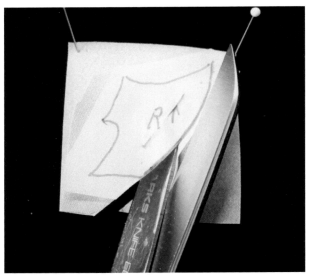
Fig. 6-8 Cut out the template.

After the shape is cut and you remove the pin the tracing paper simply falls away. You have your piece of fabric with the Steam-A-Seam 2 Lite attached to the back.

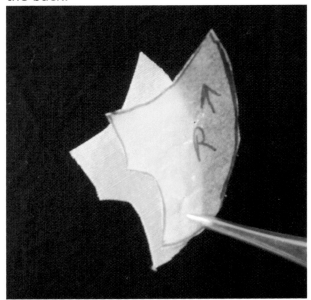
Fig. 6-9 Tracing paper template falls away

The next step is to remove the second piece of backing from the Steam-A-Seam 2 Lite. Sometimes it is necessary to start the separation of the backing from the web with the point of a pin. The webbing itself should cling nicely to the fabric once started.

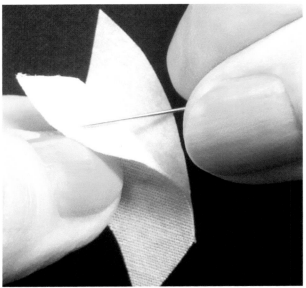
Fig. 6-10 Peel off the backing

Once the backing is removed, apply the fabric to the muslin and press into place.

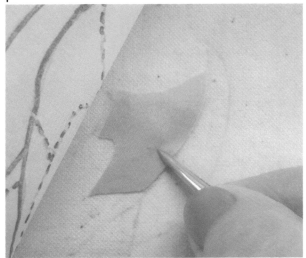
Fig. 6-11 Placing fabric onto muslin

TIP: Using a tweezer makes handling a small piece easier.

Now flip the master copy back over the quilt and check the position of the newly applied piece of fabric. If you find it is a little off position you can always lift the fabric off along with its Steam-A-Seam 2 Lite, and reapply. So long as you don't iron the Steam-A-Seam you can continue to readjust as many times as necessary.

Now that you've placed your first piece, put your second piece of tracing paper over the master copy and draw your second template. Draw this template like

Fig. 6-12 Check alignment

your first, except where it should overlap the first. Note the red arrows. They mark the edge of the underlap. Your line, at this point, should follow the drawn line on the master, not the edge of the first piece of fabric, because this line will be the exposed edge. Exposed edges always follow the lines of the mastercopy.

Fig. 6-13 Planning second piece

Place your second piece over the edge of the first aligning the rest as closely as you can to the markings on the muslin.

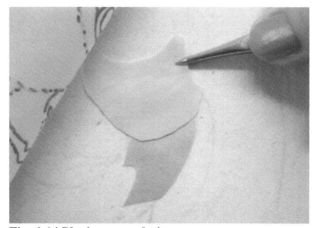

Fig. 6-14 Placing second piece

Place the mastercopy back over your fabric and make sure everything is properly aligned. Notice how at the blue arrow the edge of the second piece covers the first piece and sits exactly on the line of the mastercopy. You will notice how this second piece extends beyond the other sides of the mastercopy lines (see green arrows) to provide an underlap for the next pieces to be applied. At the red arrow there is no seam allowance because it is the edge of the face.

Fig. 6-15 Overlaps and underlaps

Chapter 7
Constructing the Face

Fig. 7-1 Judith and Holofernes

Order of Application

A question often asked is "Where do I start?" or "Which piece of fabric do I put down first?"

I like to start with the eyes. I pick the eyes for a couple of reasons. When applying fabric I think sculpturally. For example, I lay down the whites of the eye first because they are the most recessed in the face.

Depth is the illusion of perspective, of entering the picture and marching back into its recesses. As an example, let's look at my quilt *Judith and Holofernes* (Fig. 1).

Looking at this pictorial quilt, the sky at the horizon is the furthest back. Next, coming closer to us are the mountains. Closer still is Judith.

The general rule in pictorial quilting is that whatever lies *behind* or *under* gets placed first. It helps to keep this in mind when working on your quilt. In the case of *Judith and Holofernes* the sky slips *behind* the mountains. The mountain looms *in front* of the sky. Therefore, the sky is laid down first, then the mountain, and then Judith.

The depth perspective of most portrait quilts is fairly simple.

After the eyes I work out the rest of the face, then add the background, and *only then* add the hair. I do the face first because I want to choose a background that goes well with, and brings out, the subtle colors used in the face and the face's shadows. The hair goes on last because it is over both the face and the background.

In real life the rules are always bent. I said that, in general, whatever lies behind or under gets placed first, but let's analyze the portrait of Jules for examples of how the general rule is followed, and how it is bent.

Fig. 7-2 Jules

Fig.7-3 Areas to observe

Here is a portrait of Jules, my husband. Let us analyze two sections on this quilt. After laying down the purple background, I arranged the fabric sections of his face and, when satisfied with the arrangement, proceeded to do the hair. Since the hair sits on top of the skin, I put his hair in after the face (see red arrow). If you look carefully, you will note that the ear is on top of the hair at the temples (green arrow). It should go on after the hair, but if I already did the face that means that the ear must go in front of the face. That will not work. The solution to this dilemma is to gently lift the edge of the face and slip the pieces of ear fabric under the face fabric. I like to use tweezers and/or a pin for the maneuver because my fingers are too clumsy. The glasses go on last, and I use the same maneuver as before to slip the ear piece behind the ear.

As you go along with your portrait, look to see what edge should go under and what should be placed on top. If you think things out in advance you can save yourself a lot of frustration and fiddling down the road. However, there will be occasions when the general rule of thumb cannot be followed. At such times, you will have to do the same thing as I did with *Jules*. Do not worry about these exceptions because later when you thread paint you can adjust the illusion of depth.

Auditioning Fabric

Now it is time to start applying fabric. This selection process is one of the key creative parts of making your portrait quilt. I can't tell you *exactly* how you should do your quilt, or *exactly* what pieces of fabric you should use. Your choices will express your artistic vision. What I can do is give you some pointers and examples from my own work and inspire you in the process of choosing your fabric and constructing your portrait.

This section is meant to show you my thought processes as I applied the fabric to the quilt portrait *Marty* and how I dealt with the various problems that arose.

Fig. 7-4 Mastercopy of Marty

When working on Marty, I started with the eyes. Beside the reasons I gave earlier, I also like to start with the eyes because it is the "core" of the portrait. If the eyes are "right" then everything after seems to flow smoothly. Also, it contains small, difficult to handle pieces.

Fig.7-5 Photo of Marty's eyes

Marty's eyes were in deep shadow in the original photo. I could not select a pure white for the cornea. Even in a child's portrait a pure white for the cornea would be too stark, but especially here I needed to choose one that had much gray in it. I like to choose a tinted gray in most of my work—a gray with blue in it, or with green tones. If you ever choose a fabric for the cornea with a yellow tint, you have to make sure the eye will not look jaundiced.

The edges of the fabric I chose for the cornea will be covered with other fabric so I did not put any webbing on it. That accounts for those ghastly looking pins holding them in place temporarily.

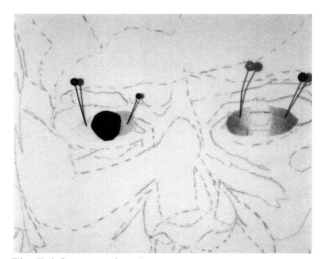

Fig. 7-6 Constructing the eyes

He has brown eyes, so I chose a dark brown for the Iris of the eye (although in the photo it appears almost black). I cut the side edges exactly as drawn on the master copy but made them a bit larger for the part that will be covered by the eyelids. I used the Steam-a-Seam 2 Lite webbing on the back of the iris fabric to hold it in place.

Then I added the black pupils. The pupil is difficult to see in this photograph. You can now see why I did not use webbing on the cornea, I was avoiding unnecessary buildup of webbing.

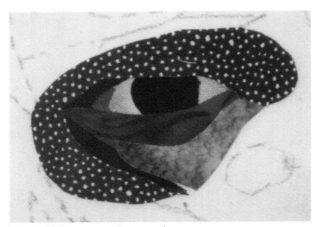

Fig. 7-7 Close up of an eye in progress

Take a look at this close up image of the eye. Notice that I chose a gray that has a slight shift in value within it. Eyeballs are round and by fussycutting I can show how they recede back into the socket. Inserting a touch of conjunctiva in the corner always adds a visceral touch of life.

I continue building out from the eyes. Laying the darker shadows down first, and keeping the lighter colors on top of them helps create a sculptural quality to the portrait.

I continued adding sections working outwards. Notice, in the so-called bag under the eye (after fussy-cutting to create a deeper shadow) I juxtaposed it against the dotted fabric, laying it on top of the other darker fabric already there. This creates an "in-depth" crease in the skin, which I will soften later with thread painting.

Do not be afraid to use two different intensities for the cornea of each eye. Notice here that the left eye's cornea is much lighter than the eye on the right (see Fig 7-8). It was less in shadow, and it would have looked terrible if I decided to make it the same color as the eye on the right just because in real life the corneas are the same color.

Fig. 7-8 Both eyes different

When composing a face, or any other art work, everything has a relationship to its neighbor that effects the whole. Even when working with "realism" one must employ "artistic privilege" to create a portrait that says more than a simple photo can say. Artistic privilege means changing something that you feel will benefit the whole work. Don't be too rigid in your choice of colors.

Fig.7-9 Building out from the eyes

Fig. 7-10 Adding 5 o'clock shadow

Ah, now things are beginning to flesh out. It starts to become more exciting to work at this point.

Although Marty assiduously shaves everyday, by mid-day his 5 o'clock shadow makes its early appearance. I have to find a piece of fabric that demonstrates this often prominent feature of his. I walk into the fabric shop and, with a grin, ask where they keep their 5 o'clock shadows. If the fabric shop is familiar with me they know exactly what I am talking about and can steer me to the perfect fabric. Otherwise, I have the fun of observing their incredulous expressions.

Notice that I do not skimp in adding details with fabric. I like to get as much of the likeness and details in before threadpainting, leaving the final touches of threadpainting for bringing the spark of life to the portrait.

Fig 7-11 Close up of mouth

Now I start the mouth. Here I have a dilemma. The part of his mouth on the left side of his lips is too narrow to handle with fabric, so I decide to leave that part of his smile to threadpainting. Of course, this means I will have to live with his lopsided mouth for quite a while. This can create a distraction whenever you have to evaluate the portrait for applying the next piece of fabric. So be it!

It is best to make the upper lip slightly darker than the bottom lip. Light strikes the lips from above, hitting the bottom lip directly, making it appear lighter than the upper lip which is turned under and away from the direct light. This gives much dimensionality to the image.

Fig. 7-12 Mouth in context

Fig. 7-13 Adding the background

Fig. 7-14 All the fabric in place

At this point Marty's face is really coming together. Before applying the hair, I add the background because the hair is going to lay on top of both the face and the background. I audition quite a few fabrics while searching for a good background piece. His expression is so intense that at first I thought I could soften the piece by using a background such as blue, or quiet green. None of that works. Then I decide that perhaps I have to find a color that "fights" with his intensity. I audition a yellow and voila! It works.

The floating head without the hair is ghastly. It makes him look like number 1 on the Ten Most Wanted List, or that he belongs in a science fiction movie entitled "The Computer Monster".

After adding the background I put in Marty's shirt. Now, still looking a bit desperate, Marty is ready to be fused and thread painted.

For comparison, here is the photograph I primarily worked from.

Fig. 7-15 Original photo

FAQ

Question:
Have you ever begun a fabric portrait with the background color pre-selected?
Answer:
Yes, but I prefer to wait until a have most of the face fabrics applied so that I can select a background that brings out the colors in those fabrics.

Question:
Is it necessary to use printed fabrics in your work, can various shades and tones of solid color produce an acceptable portrait? Also, I am having a difficult time in selecting fabric with a small scale print for skin tones of a person of color.
Answer:
Solids are okay but tend to be dull. It is recommended to use small print fabrics. Batiks are also nice, and they provide good color movement.

Question:
I am a bit confused about when and how to apply the background. Is it done at the beginning or end of the process?
Answer:
Either way is acceptable, but it is best done after the face has been completed and before the hair is applied.

Question:
Do you cut to fit the background *against* the head and body? It doesn't go under the picture does it?
Answer:
The edge of the background lies *beneath* the head and body. Abutting them might produce a gap in the final result.

Question:
Should there be a 1/4 inch margin extending all around the outside edge of our portrait when we are finished or is it to be cut right to the line?
Answer:
I assume you mean the edge of the entire work. Definitely leave a 1/4 inch margin all around. In fact I like to play safe and extend the work to 1/2 inch larger all around. Eventually, you will be squaring the work up for the application of a border or other mode of finishing. Yes, when you square it up, you TRY to keep it to the edge previously decided upon with the extra 1/4 inch beyond for attaching the border. Of course, this may not happen nicely. Hence the extra leeways.

Question:
I'm having a little bit of difficulty handling the smallest pieces of fabric. Is thread painting reserved for line work or can I "fill in" some of those tiny shadows?

Answer:
If it is a tiny shadow, yes, you can fill in with threadpainting. When considering heavily threadpainting over a fairly large area, you run the risk of its being too bulky. Also, you would want to keep a consistency throughout the whole portrait. If the major part of the portrait is very lightly threadpainted, then one heavily threaded area could stand out like a sore thumb.

Question:
I just have a simple, patterned shirt to do. The shadows on the shirt aren't that dark, the pattern of the shirt fabric still shows through where the shadows fall on the shirt. How do I show light and dark on the shirt fabric? I thought of trying to paint in some shadow (I've done very little fabric painting but could try) or fusing some translucent shadow fabric on top of the fabric of the shirt or would I use thread-painting to show the differences in light on the shirt . . . or what?

Answer:
I do not know about the shirt fabric of which you speak, but I often use the backside of a fabric for the lighter parts of the shirt and the front of the fabric for the shadows. I did this on Rundy's shirt. I also find a fabric that seems close enough in texture but is either darker than the darkest of the main fabric, and lighter than the lightest of the main fabric. That usually works.

Question:
Maybe I missed something, but the face is just placed on a piece of muslin. How do I transfer the face to a background fabric?

Answer:
I leave it on the muslin. Usually, I add the background before I add the hair. because the hair is placed over the background fabric. However, you can poke some pins through the fabric on into the foamboard to keep the hair from shifting and slip the seam allowance of the background under just a bit and fingerpress the hair down over it.

Question:
I'm really too terrified to start adding fabric. I've had time this week and actually pulled some fabric from my stash but I can't seem to take that first cut.

Answer:
You are facing what nearly every artist faces . . . that big blank white wall! Start anywhere, you can even play "Pin the tail on the donkey" to find the starting point. Keep plunging ahead, don't change anything more than 3 times. Just keep going. Remind yourself "This is only a fabric construction." No one is going to be hurt. It WILL get easier.

Chapter 8
Introduction to Threadpainting

Preparation

You've spent days putting everything together and now your quilt sits before you, ready to be fused.

Before you remove your quilt from the foamboard for fusing, it is wise to secure some of the looser sections of fabric so that nothing is knocked loose or flutters away in the process of moving. For this I use a mini iron.

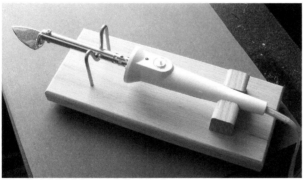

Fig. 8-1 Mini-iron with stand

A mini iron has no steam and will fuse the Steam-A-Seam 2 Lite temporarily. I apply it only in small points. If you do not have a mini iron you can use the tip of a regular iron, set to dry. Do not overdo this procedure, just secure what is needed. The dry ironing produces a weaker bond than the steam ironing you will do shortly.

For example, I might apply the mini iron to the point of a nose to hold the last bit of fabric in place, or perhaps the thin curve of an ear (see Fig. 2).

Fig. 8-2 Securing the tip of the nose

Steam Ironing

When steam ironing your quilt you can use a regular ironing board. I, however, do not like to use the average ironing board. I worry that pieces might fall off or shift. Rather than use an ironing board, I devised my own ironing board space on my dining room table.

Obviously, we never eat.

Once your ironing surface is prepared, you can call up three friends to join you in carefully lifting a designated corner of the quilt and shuffling over to lay the work neatly onto the pressing surface. Choose only well coordinated friends. Or you can do it by yourself by trying the following method:

Place board with work still on it onto the ironing surface. My board was large so I placed a chair near the table on which to rest the other end of the board.

Fig. 8-3 Preparing for transfer

Grasp two corners of the quilt and carefully slide the work until that edge sits comfortably on the ironing surface.

Fig. 8-4 Slide one edge off

With the rest of the board still under the work pin the extended edge of the quilt to hold it in place.

Fig. 8-5 Pinning to ironing surface

Slide the board out from under the rest of the quilt. The pins should hold the work in place.

Fig. 8-6 Sliding board out from under quilt

Check surface to make sure everything is in its proper place and the entire piece lies flat. Fuse the fabric to the muslin following the directions provided by Steam-a-Seam 2 Lite.

Introduction to Threadpainting

Threadpainting is how you add that last touch of detail to your portrait quilt. It is done using free motion sewing.

One of the advantages of free motion sewing is that you do not have to turn or twist the fabric around to change direction. The design is kept at 12 o'clock at all times. Your design decisions do not have to be made upside down.

Free motion sewing is used both in surface threadpainting and in quilting the final layered pieces. When threadpainting on the surface, without the weight of the batting to offer stability, I would recommend that you use a tear-away stabilizer under the fabric to keep it from bunching or pulling. A lightweight paper stabilizer such as Golden Threads Quilting Paper.

The way you sit at the sewing machine is important. You want to be comfortable and relaxed. Your elbows should be on an even level with the fabric under the needle. Resting them on the quilt not only helps you relax, but can aid in shoving the quilt along. I usually put one or two pillows on my chair seat to raise me to that even level.

The surrounding surface around the sewing machine should also be level. If you have a drop-in table for your machine, you are all set. If not, the purchase of a slip-on table surround might prove very helpful. If that is not a possibility, please rest assured that many beautifully executed free motion embellishments have been made without these amenities.

Thread Choices

There is a vast selection of thread types and sizes in the market place. There is cotton, rayon, polyester, silk, monofilament, metallic, and more. Choose thread to serve specific purposes. Each type has distinct physical properties and characteristics. Polyester (for example) retains its round shape at all times. Whereas cotton, rayon, and silk tend to lie flatter on the fabric. I would choose the latter for shading and the polyester for distinctive outlining (as it will be more raised).

Thread size plays an important role in your choice of thread. The standard size used in regular sewing is usually 40, sometimes 50. Machine embroidery uses 60 and 50. Heavy duty sewing uses number 30. Sometimes you will see the thread size shown as 50/2. The top number is the size and the bottom number is the ply (the number of filaments wound together). You will notice from the above that the larger the size number the finer the thread.

For shading I like to use number 60 (fine). With the finer thread I can go over the same area with a second color (creating a blend) without adding bulk or stiffness. However, color choice is my prime consideration, and if I cannot find the exact color I want in the finer thread I will use any weight thread with the desired color. Just adjust the stitches accordingly.

Once you have chosen your thread the first thing you need to do is set up your machine for free motion stitching.

Free Motion Checklist

1. Lower feed dogs.
2. Change to darning foot.
3. Insert Metallica or topstitch needle
4. Lower the upper tension. Tension numbers differ on different machines. The best way to find the proper tension for your machine is to play with them. You can start with your machines recommended tension for satin stitching.
5. On straight stitch selection put the stitch length at 0.
6. If you can, set the machine so that the needle stops in the down position.
7. Thread the needle.
8. Put work under needle. (Work should have stabilizer on underside.)
9. Lower needle at starting point and pull bobbin thread to top of work.
10. Re-insert needle in starting point.
11. LOWER FOOT!
12. Position hands (holding both bobbin threads firmly out of the way).
13. Say a prayer, take a deep breath and GO.

You will want to keep this checklist next to your sewing machine until the procedure becomes second nature to you.

Threadpainting Practice

Practice makes perfect.

Before you begin threadpainting your portrait quilt you should practice with other fabric until you are comfortable with the technique and feel ready to begin working on your quilt.

Start your practice with a solid colored fabric. Insert paper stabilizer under the fabric.

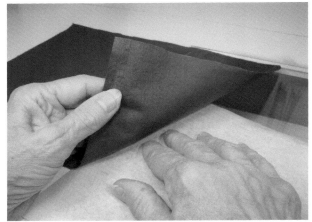

Fig. 8-7 Stabilizer goes underneath

Place fabric and stabilizer under machine and lower needle while holding onto upper thread.

Fig. 8-8 Hold upper thread

Raise needle and pull on upper thread to lift bobbin thread to top. Pull bobbin thread through all the way.

Fig. 8-9 Pull thread up

Reinsert needle into starting point. Lower foot. Hold both threads out of the way and take a few stitches in place to fix threads.

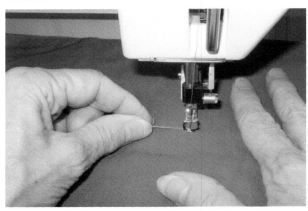

Fig. 8-10 Reinsert needle

Place both hands on sides of the fabric. Keep the fabric facing in the same direction (12 o'clock) at all times, move the fabric around. Start by making "e" loops. On the first attempt try setting the machine speed at slow and get the feel of that rhythm. Remember that your feed dogs are not pushing the fabric. You are doing that with your hands.

Fig. 8-11 Practice making "e" loops

Change the speed to medium, and then fast. Experiment to see which speed is best for your movements. The trick is to keep an even speed and an even, steady movement. I use different speeds for different purposes.

Now try writing your name.(I hope yours is better than mine.)

Fig. 8-12 Write your name

The feathery stitch is good for feathery edges, fill-ins, and shading. I usually set my machine at fast speed for this. The pattern is made by moving the fabric back and forth fairly quickly while pressing steadily on the foot pedal.

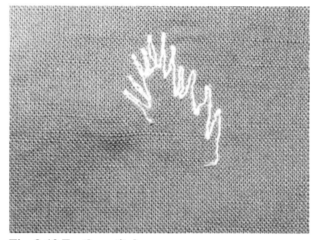

Fig. 8-13 Feather stitch

If at any time you feel tense or nervous, or cannot decide in which direction to continue (due to the brain being slower than the machine, like mine) take your foot off pedal immediately and stop. Do not try to outrace the machine. Sometimes starting off again in the middle of a task can be tricky. Decide the trail you want to follow and press your foot all the way to continue. It takes a little practice, but then, that is what you are doing.

You can set your machine for zig-zag with free motion sewing to produce interesting effects. Just make sure the width you select allows your needle to fit within the darning foot opening. Leave the stitch length at "0". Move your fabric straight, diagonally, or create a circle and see what happens.

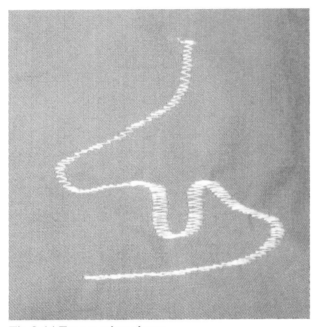

Fig.8-14 Free motion zigzag

For your second practice piece, choose a fabric with a large flower print.

Trace around the edges, fill in with the feathery stitch, and practice the running stitch. The running stitch is the same as straight stitching, however, here you will be doing it with free motion sewing, allowing you to move diagonally, sideways, and in

Fig. 8-15 Threadpaint the flower

curves. You used the running stitch when you wrote your name.

If your machine has a variety of stitches available, play with them. Always make sure the design is not too wide for the foot.

The feathery stitch is good for indicating hair, as in this detail below of a beard from *Mordechai and Esther*.

Fig. 8-16 Featherstitching a beard

Although I use a lot of free motion sewing, the major part of all my portraits have been done with an applique foot and ordinary zig-zag sewing. This is partly because I am a control freak. Ordinary zig-zag stitching gives me greater control of my stitches, and looks neater, calling less attention to itself. You would be surprised at how much variety you can get with "just plain zig-zag". There are areas, though, where free-motion stitching is a must, such as the eyes and the hair. Highlighting certain areas, such as the moistness of lips and light shining on a wave of hair, is best

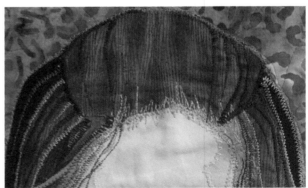

Fig. 8-17 Free-motion stitching on hair

done with free motion stitching.

Zig-zag differs ever so slightly from satin-stitching. Visually, satin stitch gives a neater but more definitive edge to the stitching. The zig-zag produces a more open and softer look. I use both, but I do have a preference for the zig-zag. I think it looks more arty, whereas the satin stitch looks more finished, like a baseball cap logo. If you lengthen (open) the satin stitch, it looks nicer.

Practice zigzagging while changing the width of the stitch (example on right in photo below). Also try changing the length at the same time as the width (example on left below).

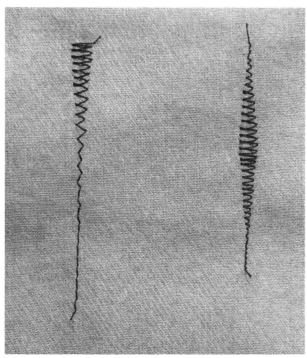

Fig. 8-18 Varying the zigzag stitches

If you are not ambidextrous (it takes time to be that), you can stop and change the controls and then continue. Go around curves. Make points (like arrows), in general play with the stitches and observe the results.

If your machine has decorative stitches, play with those. But this time ask yourself questions like: "Does this stitch resemble hair?" "Would that stitch help me make a jagged edge when stitching a flower?"

Practice these steps a little every day. Even to this day, every time I am ready to start threadpainting an art quilt, I sit down and practice in order to loosen up and set a rhythm.

Chapter 9
Threadpainting

Threadpainting Your Quilt: Overview

Before you begin threadpainting your quilt I advise taking scrap pieces of fabric from your work and placing them on a piece of muslin using fusible web as before. You will use this to audition thread colors, try different stitches and, in general, do your experimentation on this piece instead of the actual artwork. You will avoid a lot of heartache that way.

When I sit down to threadpaint, I usually start in the center of the work and work my way out to the sides, and then either up and out or down and out. Starting from the center helps prevent fabric bubbles from forming. When I work up and out, I try to finish the upper half of the work entirely before tackling the other half. I feel much more secure rolling up an already threadpainted section for slipping under the machine than rolling the side which has not been secured by threads. Sometimes, as you work you will find areas of applique that seem to be loosening. Even if it is on the other side of the work, I threadpaint that piece immediately.

For economy of labor, I try to thread paint as much as I can using the same color thread that may be required within the area I am working on before changing the thread.

If you have a machine that fixes the beginning and ending stitches permanently, then you can just cut them off and not bother to pull the ends to the back. However, make sure that the ending stitches will not create an ungainly group of stitches that interfere with the flowing delicacy of the artwork.

When the threads on the front begin to annoy me, I either thread a needle and pull them to the back that way, or sometimes, if the area is not heavily threadpainted I just tug on the end stitch of the thread on the back and pull it to the back. I do not bother to secure it with a knot, because it does get sewn over enough to secure it. Loose thread ends are not important to me because they will be hidden in the quilt sandwich. I pull the threads to the back from both the start and the end of a line of stitches.

Whether you are thread painting a face, a tree, or a house, the principles are the same. I would use matching thread and zig-zag the edge down for most of the work, leaving free motion embellishment for areas such as shading, emphasis, detail, and highlights. I like to secure the entire piece as quickly as possible, which is why I leave the detail stitching for later.

When working, I do not cover the entire back of the work with tear away stabilizer at one time. I use a piece of stabilizer just large enough to cover the area I am thread painting. As soon as I finish that area I remove the stabilizer. If I left it, it would become more difficult to remove later. If a small piece of stabilizer remains on the back because it has become threaded too tightly, do not worry. It has no effect on the feel of the wallhanging.

I use a very lightweight stabilizer that is paper and tears easily. To remove the stabilizer, I use tweezers to grab the paper to start the tear. I slip one point of the tweezers under the paper and run it sideways (blunt edge) along the edge of the stitching pulling the stabilizer up and back towards the direction of the tear with my other hand. If you use a heavier weight stabilizer that does not tear crisply, then you may have to cut it away. Sometimes I remove some of the larger pieces that get left behind with tweezers. For this, I place my fingers lightly on top of the stitches to keep them from warping and pull the paper out and away from the stitching with the tweezers. I do not try to dig out small pieces from between the stitches.

I prefer to do my embellishments (details, highlighting, etc,) before quilting because I do not like the look of the back of the quilt when embellishment is applied through all three layers of the quilt. This is just my preference. If you want to use the embellishment for quilting through the batting, you should encounter no problems different than you might with ordinary free motion quilting. You will need to change the way you pull threads to the back since the threads should be hidden. You will have to weave the threads into the batting layer.

Threadpainting: Detailed Instruction

While working, place the original photograph near your machine for reference. Also keep on hand that piece of muslin with fabric scraps that you created.

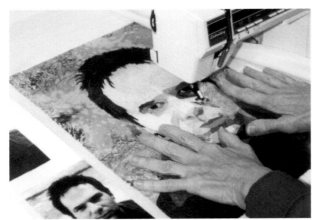
Fig. 9-1 Original photo at hand

You will continue to use that to test out thread colors and try stitch possibilities on it.

Fig. 9-2 Scraps of fabric fused to muslin

Sometimes I keep other photographs of the person handy, but you must be careful because each picture will have different colorations.

The Eyes

Sometimes the figure in your portrait will have large eye-brows which can be created (in part) with a section of fabric.

Fig. 9-3A Well defined eyebrows

Fig. 9-3B Fabric pieces used for eyebrows

Other portraits have fine brows that must be done entirely in threadpainting.

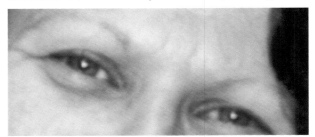
Fig. 9-4 Original photo of Fran's thin brows

In the case of the portrait of my daughter Frances, it seems I have covered the eyebrow line with fabric.

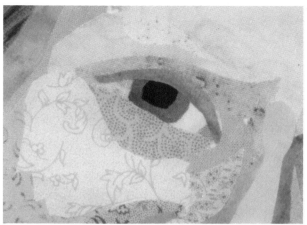

Fig. 9-5 Missing eyebrow

I do not want to mark the fabric with pencil or even washable markers. Hopefully I will never wash this quilt. So, to determine where I should threadpaint this eyebrow I place a piece of tracing paper over the eyebrow section of the master copy (still lying around somewhere, I hope). Trace the eyebrows using the Sharpie ultra fine pen.

Do not use a pencil as it will rub off on the thread. Also trace some of the eye to help you situate the eyebrow properly onto the fabric.

Fig. 9-6 Retrace eyebrows

Fig. 9-7 Place over quilt and pin to hold

Using thread that matches the skin, stitch a simple scant outline of the eyebrows only.

Fig. 9-8 follow outline

Tear away the tracing paper. Since you used a simple running stitch, it should remove easily. What you are left with will serve as a guide.

Eyebrows should be done with free motion stitching. My daughter Frances has thin eyebrows. Using a feather-like stitch, I made the stitches slant in the direction that hairs grow.

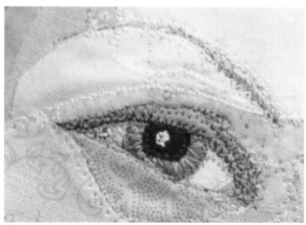

Fig. 9-9 Threadpainted eyebrow

I used free motion sewing to highlight the iris. No iris is simply blue or brown. There are flecks of color radiating out like spokes from the pupil of the eye.

Eyes come to life when light reflections are shown in the pupil. Sometimes there are two reflections, one perhaps slightly smaller than the other, such as in the portrait of my granddaughter Rachel.

Fig. 9-10 Two highlights in Rachel's eyes

Sometimes a photograph will not show the reflected light in a person's eye, such as the case with Marty. His eyes were in such deep shadow that I had to invent the white spots. You should make sure your eyes have these bits of reflected light–otherwise the eyes will seem dead.

Fig.9-11 Marty's eyes

Different eyes will require slightly different work. As a second example there is the case of Marty. Below is a photograph of one of Marty's eyes, both before threadpainting and afterward.

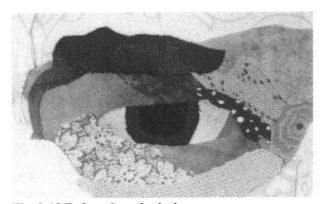
Fig. 9-12 Before threadpainting

Fig. 9-13 After Threadpainting

Note in this detail (Fig. 9-13) you can see how I threadpainted the iris, creating the spokes of color. This was a good chance for me to lighten the darkness of the brown I chose by choosing a brown thread that is slightly lighter. If a person's eyes are blue/gray, this would be a good time to bring out the dominant color, or intimate the secondary color.

I then added the dash of white highlight, but I did not actually use a straight white, instead, using a gray to subdue it. After all, the eyes were in shadow. The cornea space seemed too flat, so I added more depth with a few zig-zag stitches toward the corners, especially on the upper part of the exposed cornea just below the upper lid. The upper lid casts a shadow on the eye, and darkening the areas just below (very subtly) brings the eyelid forward and over the eye. I like to emphasize the upper lid with a darker thread than the lower lid. If you look back at Fran's eye you will note that I also added a thin line of red along the lower lid to give it depth.

On *Marty*, the eyebrows just seemed to sit there like a heavy blob of color. They needed a bit more airiness and lightness. First I stitched (the feather stitch) in the center of the eyebrow with a lighter brown thread. Using a thread that matched the forehead, I created the illusion of being able to see the forehead through the hairs of the eyebrows, thereby making them look airier. I did the same with the underside of the brow, this time using a lighter thread than the neighboring skin tone, giving the brows an extra "lift". I also chose a pink hue to tie it in with the other surrounding skins.

Tip: Do not try to add long eyelashes to your portrait. It never works.

By this time the back of your quilt is beginning to look like a mess of threads.

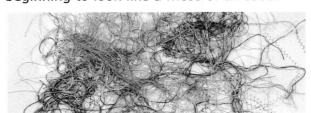
Fig. 9-14 A mess of threads

Have no fear. As I mentioned earlier, this mess will lie between the batting and the top undetected. Most of the threads get stitched over and will not shift around.

Joining Skin Sections

Note: Always remember to have every edge of fabric covered with stitching so that the pieces will never fall off or fray.

When stitching two sections of skin fabric together try to soften edges. Usually choosing the thread that matches the ligher-toned fabric produces a less harsh effect (red arrow).

Fig. 9-15 Threadpainting skin joins on *Frances*

If you want to emphasize an edge, such as the laugh line (green arrow) use a darker thread. For true emphasis you can run one or two lines of straight stitching in a similar but darker color, such as was done for the nostrils (blue arrow).

Always use black sparingly. When you cannot get darker in a color, then okay. The same applies to white. There should be a mere one or two strokes of intense white or black to enliven a design. To much and it loses its dynamics.

Do not overdo. It is very difficult to diminish a mistake that has too many threads. Remember that you can always add that little detail you are contemplating later on. Each section you add has its effect on the others. Get the basic tones and edges done all over before working on minute details. This also helps you control the mood of the portrait. If you are beginning to think of adding black, you know for sure it is time to move on.

The Nose

Treat the edges of the nose much as you would other skin joins, avoiding strong dark demarcations, except for the nostrils, which should be delineated strongly (see red arrow in Fig. 16).

Notice the single row of stitching delineating the edge of the nares (Blue arrow). By emphasizing the edge in this manner, the nose comes forward.

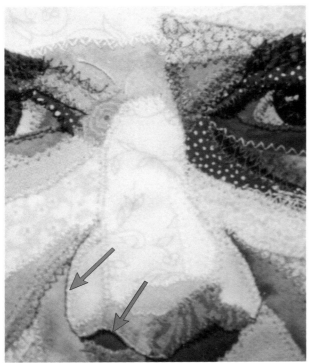

Fig. 9-16 Marty's nose

The Mouth

Remember how I had to live with Marty's lopsided smile when I was piecing together the fabric of his portrait? Well, now I can confront it and fix it with thread painting. I don't want to rely on finding the right position of the smile while I am in the middle of stitching, so I trace a template, using the same method I employed with Frances' eyebrows, and then stitched the

Fig. 9-17 Marty's lips before threadpainting

line in.

It is all right to use red for a man's lips if the rest of the portrait can deal with it. If the colors of the portrait are strong, then they can counterbalance the use of red lips for a man. However, as you will note in the thread painted lips of Marty (see Fig. 9-18), I tempered the red by softening the outlines of the lips. On the upper lip I used thread matching the skin. On the bottom lip I used a lighter red, or pink. If I hadn't tempered them, the lips would take on too strong an outline and look more like lipstick. I loose squiggled some shadows in at the ends of the smile, giving them depth.

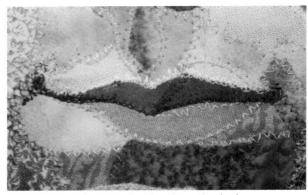

Fig. 9-18 Lip is extended by threadpainting

If your portrait has an open smile you will need to stitch the teeth. The trick to stitching teeth is to avoid demarcating each tooth heavily. Proceed to make a tracing in the same manner as for the eyebrows. Trace the lips as well.

Fig. 9-19 Trace teeth and lips

Fig. 9-19B Pin to face

Pin tracing paper to face, aligning everything carefully. On top of the tracing paper, straight stitch the lines for the teeth with white thread. Tear off paper.

This is an area where free motion stitching comes in handy. You have already used white thread to demarcate the teeth. Stitch the gums next. The only part of the gums that are showing are the little triangle shaped areas below the top lip. Fill them in imitating a satin stitch.

Starting with thin thread (size 60) just a shade deeper than white, and using a running stitch, stitch halfway up the length

Fig. 9-20 Detail of gums

of the teeth next to the canines. If stitching back down would make the shading too heavy, then end that row of stitching. Pull the thread to the back, and continue shading the teeth as they disappear into the back of the smile, changing to darker hues as needed. You cannot be lazy here. It requires a bit of fussy stitching, but the effort is worth it. Be very light-handed with the teeth. Do not overdo.

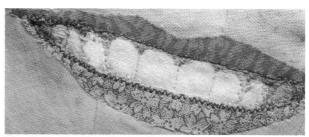

Fig. 9-21 Shading the teeth

If you're doing this you're probably wishing you chose a face with no smile. Have no fear, it will look nice. Just remember to go slowly, keep it simple, and be light-handed. It is always better to under-do.

The Hair

For the hair I use both free motion and tapering zig-zag stitches. Where the hair grows out of the forehead, use free motion sewing, employing the feather stitch. The tapered zig-zag works well for loose strands of hair. It is nice to make the strand of hair stand out more by choosing a lighter color thread than the color of the fabric. Then, in a darker tone, you can sew a running stitch along the edge of the strand.

Fig. 9-22 Rachel's hair

Fig. 9-23 Marty's spiky hair

Clothing

Fig. 9-24 Threadpainting a collar

When working on clothing, pay attention to highlights and shadows. In the above example, notice how in Fig. 24 the edge of the collar is highlighted by adding a line of zigzag in an off-white thread (blue arrow). I also tried to bring the collar forward further by running a single row of stitches with a darker thread along the outer edge of the collar within the shadow of the shirt (green arrow).

Notice how the illusion of depth created by the addition of a darker thread along the edge of a fold (see Fig 25, red arrow). At the yellow arrow you can see a softer shadow along the fold created by using a thread darker, but close to the fabric adjacent to the fold.

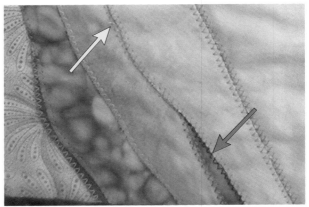

Fig. 9-25 Threadpainting fold edge

In general, follow the procedure of using light and dark threads along edges to create a natural three-dimensional effect. Lighter edges come forward and darker edges recede.

Finished

And there you have it! Threadpainting adds that vital detail and spark of life to your portrait quilt. With threadpainting completed, your quilt is almost finished.

FAQ

Question:

What do you use in the bobbin? Is it okay to just stick with invisible thread in the bobbin for everything or do you use a neutral cotton thread?

Answer:

I use the same thread in the bobbin as I have up above. It insures an even look (nothing unwanted peeping through).

Question:

What is the best way to do glasses? Treat the glasses shape as an integral part of the whole pattern like any other shape, or complete the whole eye area first an then do the glasses as an overlay?

Answer:

You can threadpaint the thin ones in. I did this with Morris. Thick rims (such as horn-rimmed) require fabric.

Question:

How do I do the white points of light? Are they fabric, thread, paint?

Answer:

The twinkle in the eye is added with threadpainting.

Question:

Can I use variegated thread on the skin?

Answer:

Variegated thread is risky, it could vary in an area that you don't want it to vary, and to a shade that shouldn't be.

Question:

Wouldn't it be easier to just use some fancy stitches (if your sewing machine has them) to connect the fabric pieces, except those that really require a more painted look?

Answer:

If they are appropriate to achieve the effect you want, absolutely use them.

Chapter 10
Finishing the Quilt

Now that you have a beautiful top, it is time to put the finishing touches on it. You can mount it on stretchers, then frame it and call it Art (media: fabric). Or follow the traditional definition of a quilt, that a quilt consist of three layers: a backing, batting and a top. The main difference being that as art you can charge over $20,000 for it and as a quilt, well, there are very few quilt artists who can command that kind of money. Besides, who can count money with sore fingers?

Instead, we are going to spend money on an appropriate fabric for the backing.

In addition to looking for a color that compliments the front and brings out the flavors of its colors, we want to choose a fabric print that carries with it the same ambience and emotions found in the artwork.

If you are insecure about producing nice even stitching with free-motion quilting, then hunt for a somewhat busy pattern for the back fabric. The stitching is harder to see (this is supposedly an old seadog's trick).

Traditional quilts usually require some degree of loft. This is not so with a portrait quilt. Too much puffiness can distort the features. When purchasing batting, I look for whatever will produce the least loft. I very often use one or two layers of flannel as batting.

Quilting A Face

My over-careful nature dictates that I prepare *Marty* for becoming a quilt in the time-honored, safest way possible. Well, maybe it is also that I hate to deal with pins all over the place, and I am leery of slippage with temporary adhesive methods.

My backing is cut a little larger than the top. I tape this down first, right side facing the table, securing it nicely but avoiding stretching it. Then I add the batting, also taped into place on top of the backing. Finally I center the top on the layers, securing it in the same manner. I baste first diagonally from center to corners, then center to edges keeping my rows fairly close.

Fig. 10-1 Marty taped and basted to table

After removing all the tape with whichever fingers are not sore, I am ready to quilt.

I use monofilament thread in both the bobbin and as an upper thread. If you prefer not to use monofilament thread in both the bobbin and needle you can use very thin lingerie thread in the bobbin and monofilament for the upper thread. Also, for the upper thread you can use cotton thread that matches the fabric you are stitching on at the moment. This would entail changing the upper thread often and might interfere with the look of fluidity that quilting should have. This can be overcome with very careful matching of stitches at the beginning and end of lines.

I make sure my machine is well cleaned and cared for before starting to quilt. Sometimes, to help the quilt glide smoothly across the table, I spray the table top with a silicon spray. This can be purchased in the hardware section of your local store. I bought mine in the House Paint department. Always follow the directions on the can. I spray the surface of the table and let it dry. If I feel I sprayed too heavily, I wipe off the excess.

I also swipe the needles with a liquid such as Sewer's Aid to prevent gummy buildup. Sewer's Aid is silicon that comes in a small plastic bottle, and can be purchased at most fabric stores or ordered by catalogue. Make sure when you apply it to the needle that you clear out the needle's eye with the tip of a Needle Threader or pin.

Set your machine the same as you did for threadpainting.

If your backing fabric is dark, insert smoke monofilament into the bobbin. For the top, you will be changing from clear to smoke as needed.

You might want to play with the tensions of both top and/or bottom threads. Experiment on that quilt sandwich you made in earlier before sewing on the real thing. I keep an extra bobbin case on hand for playing with the bottom tension. I leave the original bobbin case always in its pristine state. You can mark the second bobbin case with nail polish, acrylic paint (using a very, very fine brush) or the Ultrafine Sharpie pen (jewelers use it, it stays on metal without smearing). Mark the bobbin case's starting

points before turning the screws. Then you can find your way back.

On the following photo of the bobbin you can see where I marked the indentation for the screwdriver with the same color as its starting point. Otherwise, I would not remember which end matches the starting point.

Fig. 10-2 Marked bobbin case

When winding monofilament onto a bobbin, use slow speed. Monofilament can stretch slightly. Then, after being sewn, it may relax (shrink back to shape), pulling the fabric slightly.

Always pull the bobbin thread up to the top of all the layers when starting a new line of stitching. If left on the back of the layers during free motion quilting, the bobbin thread might jam and bobble. If this happens, cut away the mess, and start a new line, continuing from a few stitches back and stitching forward over the place where the break occurred.

If you still have space available on your testing piece of muslin covered with fabric scraps, layer it with batting and backing like your main work. Do not bother to baste as it is only for continued experimentation. You will practice speeds, and motifs (such as meandering) before actually quilting them onto the portrait. Keep it at your side by the machine. If you do not have that piece anymore, make a decent little quilt sandwich of two pieces backing with batting in between.

Always warm up, rhythm-wise, when changing motifs.

Whenever changing upper thread

and/or bobbin thread, test it on that practice quilt to make sure it sews smoothly.

Where To Quilt

It does not matter how thin the batting (even if you use just flannel), there will always be some slight puffing along the stitch lines. Therefore you must plan what parts of the face to quilt on that will look like natural contours. A good general rule is to quilt where you have applied dark thread painting (in the shadows). Dark indicates a receding form. Light is on the outer parts, like the tip of the nose.

Working from the center out whenever possible, stitch under the eyebrows and possibly down part of the edge of the nose (only where the nose shadows are deep). For quilting the lower edge of the eyebrows, you can apply a form of feather stitch similar to the one you used during threadpainting. The red lines in the pictures below show where the quilt stitching has been done.

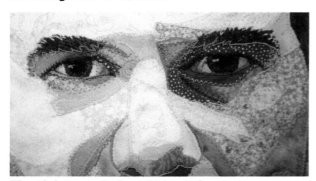

Fig. 10-3 Example from Marty's face

Then stitch the lips.

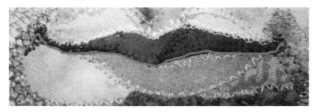

Fig. 10-4 Marty's lips

Then the rest of the person.

Fig. 10-5 Entire Quilt

For the clothing, I followed the folds of the garment.

In the background, I added a very tight meandering stitch, which helped project the head forward Under the collar of his jacket called for the same meandering stitch.

In the border on Marty's portrait, I echoed the general pattern of the fabric. You can use any pattern that pleases you on your border. For example, you can make a more open meandering stitch. There is also the possibility of meandering loops. Remember the e-loops you practiced? Just have them roam around all over the place. My only recommendation is to keep the pattern fluid. Geometric, sharp angular quilting would not be in keeping with the fluid movement on the portrait proper. I would run a stitch in the ditch between the portrait and the border to divide them.

Always try to keep the quilting on the face to a minimum.

For clothing, it usually is best to follow the folds, or echo the print of the fabric. When following the folds, stitch in the depth of them, the dark part.

The fabric in Rachel's dress had a wonderful pattern that looked like folds. I stitched in the recesses of the pattern and followed the edges of the ruffles.

You can quilt tightly anywhere, except on the face, skin or hair.

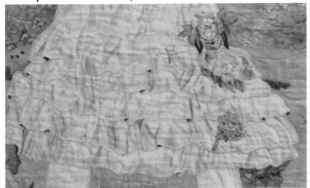

Fig. 10-6 Fabric patterns make good folds to follow

Finishing The Background

The background can meander, echo the pattern of the fabric as in Fig. 8, or

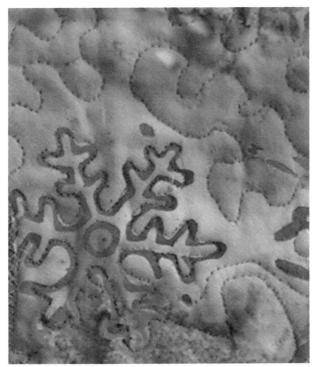

Fig. 10-7 Combined meander and outline stitch

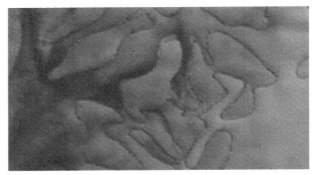

Fig. 10-8 Outlining the pattern

combine the two as in the example in Fig. 7.

In Frances' jacket (Fig. 9) I created a quilting pattern by following the direction of the petals as I stitched from flower center to flower center.

In Fig. 10 I stitched a horizontal wavy pattern for the earth, and outlined the round stones.

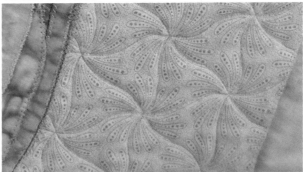

Fig. 10-9 Creating a quilted jacket

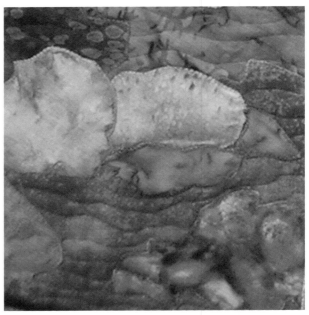

Fig. 10-10 Quilting earth and stones

In general when quilting your work analyze the rest of the portrait and ask yourself: should I emphasize the main object, or should I go with the flow? If you decide to go with the flow, then you could choose, for example, a widely spaced stitch that echoes the form of the subject.

The example below from *Miriam's Dance* I wanted to create the effect of radiating energy from her dance, so I chose wavy lines which followed her movements.

Fig. 10-11 Radiating movement

To accentuate the movement of the dance I quilted the flow of her body as seen in the neck and arms.

When doing glasses, stitch around the eyeglasses, but not on the lenses. Any stitching inside the lens would create dimensionality and it would look like the lens had fallen out.

When finished quilting, true the project up and add the trim as you would with a traditional quilt.

Label Your Quilt

One should get into the habit of making a label to place on the back of the quilt. This should contain the name of the quilt, the date it was made, and the name of its creator. It is good practice to sew this into the binding. Also make a second label with your name and address to put into the other corner of the back, but do not secure it into the binding as you may have to remove it. Labels sewn into the binding cannot be removed easily, which helps deter any would-be thieves.

You can make a very nice label using your computer and printer. Take some freezer paper, and cut a piece ½" larger than a piece of standard paper. Standard paper measures 8 ½" x 11", so the piece you cut should measure 9" x 11 ½".

Next you take the piece of the fabric you chose for the label and soak it in Bubble Jet Set according to the package directions. Bubble Jet Set is a liquid that prepares the fabric for inkjet printing, making it permanent. When dry, press out any wrinkles and iron the freezer paper (waxed side) to the back of the fabric (Fig 12). Do not use steam.

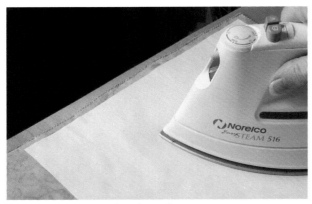

Fig. 10-12 Ironing fabric to freezer paper

Trim off the ¼" allowance on all sides to bring it to standard paper size (Fig 13). Trimming it after ironing the paper and fabric together provides a clean edge, making it easier to travel through the printer. You want to be absolutely sure there are no hanging threads that can catch in the printer!

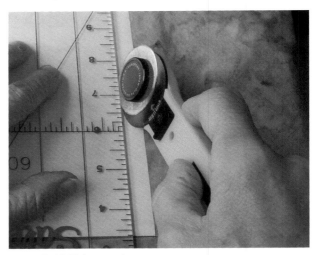

Fig. 10-13 Trim to size

Design your labels using your computer software. You can easily fit both labels onto one page for printing. Hand feed the fabric/paper through the printer, making sure the printing is done on the fabric side. You will want to do a practice run to be sure you are printing on the right side and that your lettering is coming out in the right direction.

Then divide the piece into separate labels. If you use a rotary cutter that you have set aside for paper and your ruler, you will get a square edge for both labels. Peel off the freezer paper.

Fig. 10-14 Printed label

Turn under three edges, leaving one edge extended to tuck under the binding. Since the labels are placed on opposite sides of the back, make sure the unhemmed edges are not on the same side.

Fig. 10-15 Three edges turned under

Baste label onto lower side edge of back leaving ample space away from the bottom of the quilt. This allows for easier mitering of corners. The unturned edge sits along the edge of the quilt, but leaves just a touch of the quilt to show beneath it for a more accurate edge and easier turning of the binding.

Fig. 10-16 Baste label to edge

Hanging Your Quilt

Since this is strictly a wall hanging, you will want to add a hanging sleeve on the back top edge. A sleeve is a tunnel made of fabric through which a bar or wooden dowel is passed. The sleeve is made as a tunnel so the rod does not touch the quilt and there is no chance that your quilt will be damaged by oils or other materials that might come off the rod. A hole or hook of some sort can be added on each end of the bar/dowel. Even though the portrait is small in size, the sleeve opening should be at least 4" wide. This is a requirement at most quilt shows.

The sleeve should be basted in place before you apply the binding. It should be sewn in with the binding to add stability and strength to it.

Cut a piece of fabric 8 ½" x 1" shorter than the width of your quilt. Some people use muslin. I like to use the same fabric that I used for the backing. This makes the sleeve virtually invisible. Fold in half along the long edge with right sides together.

Fig. 10-17 Fold in half along length

Place sleeve with raw edges along top edge. Once again, as with the labels, leave an eensy bit of the edge of the quilt showing along top edge. This makes for a more exact ½" seam as seen from the front. It also makes for a less bulky section for turning. After all, you are adding two extra layers to the quilt, and where the sleeve ends there will be a slight difference in thickness. This camouflages the difference just a little bit. Make sure the sleeve has even space between it and the sides of the quilt.

Baste it to the quilt approximately ¼" in from the top (the white basting in photo below). I stitch the binding to the quilt (½" from edge) through all the layers of the quilt.

Fig. 10-18 Only top is basted for now

Leave the sides and bottom unbasted for now. Apply binding in your favorite method.

After finishing the binding, fold up the sleeve so that it sits no further than halfway way up the width of the top binding.

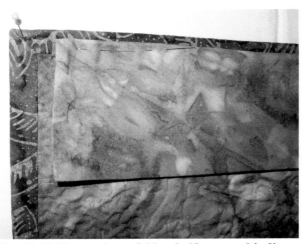

Fig. 10-19 Create sleeve fold to half-way up binding

Pin in place. Then hemstitch the bottom of the sleeve, leaving the sides open. Unpin the top. This will make the sleeve blouse slightly in the back, helping the quilt to lie flat in the front when a round dowel or pipe (as used in shows) is passed through. The reason you fold it up no further than half the width of the binding is that you do not want the sleeve to show from the front.

Now you're done. I hope this book has opened up a new world in quilting for you. To see more of my work, and work done by my students continue on to the next chapter.

Good luck quilting!

Chapter 11
Gallery of Quilts

My Parents is the first portrait quilt I created. I made it from a black and white photograph taken by my daughter Frances. It gave me great joy constructing this quilt because as I put the portrait together it was as if my parents were alive again. My parents were hard working people and never got to travel much. I like to think that as this quilt has been shown around the country they are finally getting their chance to see the world.

My Parents
1999
26 ¼" x 20 ½"

Rachel
2000
36 ½" x 44 ½"

Jules
2001
15 ¼″ x 20 ½″

Marty
2002
17 ¾" x 22 ¾"

Frances
2002
21 ½" x 24 ¼"

Morris

2004
24" x 25 "

Rundy
2004
41" x 51"

Student Quilts

Here is a selection of quilts done by some of my students. My profuse apologies to all of my students who did such excellent work but were omitted because of space constraints. I wish I could have included you all.

LaRetta Trower

Libby Mire

Mary Richling

Paula Coleman

Bonnie Keller

Sonya DeMonner

Student Quilts

Mary Manahan

Cecile Yadro

Fran Goldberg

Lorry Chwazik

Jeanne Gray

Brigitte Otto

About the Author

Born in Brooklyn, Marilyn Belford left a successful New York City painting career to retire in upstate New York. It was then she discovered art quilting. Drawing on her artistic background and her love for quilting, she developed a simple technique to create beautiful fabric portraits.

Marilyn Belford's art quilts have appeared nationwide, from American Quilter's Society in Paducah to the International Quilt Festival in Houston, Texas. Her work has won many top awards. In 2004, Marilyn was nominated for The Professional Quilter "teacher of the year" award, and was also nominated for the New York Quilters Consortium's Achievement Award. Marilyn has published an article on realistic portraits in *Quilting Today*. Her quilts have also appeared in *Quilter's Newsletter*, *Quilting Quarterly* and *Fons and Porter's Love of Quilting*.

At Quilt University (www.quiltuniversity.com) she has taught students who lived as far away as Alaska, Australia and Germany. She continues to display her quilts nationally in shows while lecturing and teaching classes, and giving courses online at Quilt University.

Her work, as well as that of some of her students, can be found at www.marilynbelford.com.

CPSIA information can be obtained
at www.ICGtesting.com
Printed in the USA
LVIW021431021012

301197LV00006B